pompom

K-N-I-T H-O-W

SIMPLE KNITS, TOOLS & TIPS

Knit How – Simple Knits, Tools, & Tips
Published in 2018 by Pom Pom Press
Text and Illustrations © 2018 Pom Pom Press

ISBN: 978-0-9934866-9-2

A catalogue record for this book is available from
the British Library.

Editors:	Meghan Fernandes & Lydia Gluck
Managing Editor:	Amy Collins
Copywriter:	Sophie Scott
Studio Managers:	Iesha Parker & Gayle Taliaferro Gilner
Project Assistant:	Alice Sleight
Design & Layout:	Bless
Pattern Design:	Meghan Fernandes, Lydia Gluck, Fiona Alice, Francesca Hughes
Sample Knitters:	Meghan Fernandes, Lydia Gluck, Rebecca Yohe, Francesca Hughes, Fiona Alice, Alice Sleight, Juliet Jung, Sophie Scott, Amy Collins
Pattern Photography:	Amy Gwatkin
Tutorial Photography:	Laura Morsman
Technical Editors:	Laura Chau & Jemima Bicknell
Copy Editors:	Annie Prime & Francesca Baldry
Models:	Roshni Gambier, Ayesha McMahon, Issa Sissoko, Gayle Taliaferro Gilner
Hair & Makeup:	Jenny Green
With thanks to:	Juju Vail, Hill Country Weavers & Rachel Atkinson.

For pattern corrections, please visit:
pompommag.com/errata

Printed in the UK by Pureprint Group Limited

POM POM PRESS
C005 Lighthouse Space
89A Shacklewell Lane
London E8 2EB
United Kingdom

pompommag.com

CONTENTS

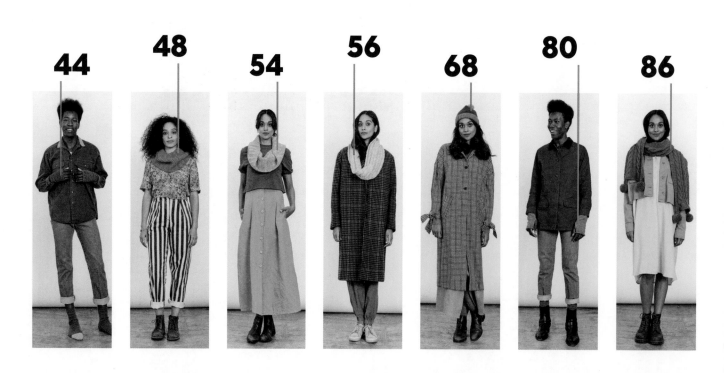

A download code for the digital edition of this book can be found on the inside of the back cover.

93   98   106   110   124   134   170

INTRODUCTION

Yay! You are reading this book! That means that A) you have a very clever friend who bought it for you, or B) you are very clever and bought it as a treat for yourself. If it was A, lucky you. You have yourself a knitting pal! Knitting pals are the best pals (if we do say so ourselves). And if you're a B, you're still lucky; pretty soon you're going to have a whole bevy of knitting friends. You might find these friends at your local yarn or coffee shop, or you might find them through the magic of the world wide web. Either way, you'll find that knitters are some of the most approachable, friendly, talented, resourceful people in the world. And guess what? Now you're one of them!

Or shall we say "one of us"? For we are knitters, and we have written this book just for you. Who are we? We're Meghan and Lydia, and we run a knitting magazine called *Pom Pom Quarterly*. We love knitting, and we love our knitting pals so much we thought there should be many, many more of them. We also thought that these new knitters might like a really straightforward, plain-talkin' and, frankly, stylish book to learn the ways of the modern knitter.

We've taught a lot of new knitters and we remember when we were new knitters too - neither of us was one of those lucky kiddos who learned from their mum or grandmother at a wee age - so we hope that we can be of help to you now. We'll be here, holding your hand and looking over your shoulder as you make those first few shaky stitches. And we'll be here as you grow in confidence and take on more exciting challenges with each new project!

Nothing feels better than sending a new knitter off on their own magical creative journey, so thanks for letting us be a part of yours. Now let's get knitting!

Meghan & Lydia
xoxo

Part 1

USEFUL THINGS TO KNOW

OK, deep breath - we're jumping in. A few things to remember before we get started:

1. Practice!

You're going to want to do some practice knitting before you start a proper project. This means taking some yarn and needles and faffing around until said yarn looks like knitting. This might take a little while. Throw your perfectionist tendencies out the window for the time being; your knitting is probably not going to look very pretty to start with. There will likely be holes, it'll doubtless be uneven, but it'll get better, we promise. This is all about practice. And as we always say: being bad at something is the first step to being really good at something!

2. Knitting is made up of two main building blocks: the knit stitch and purl stitch.

Knitting is kind of like a code or a language. In knitting, there are only really two building blocks (or words, if we're going with the language metaphor). These two building blocks are the knit stitch and the purl stitch. All knitting is basically a combination of or variation on these two stitches. Once you've got these two simple stitches down, the world is your oyster! (An oyster with a purl instead of a pearl.)

3. How to get your supplies.

You can find a knitting friend to borrow needles and yarn from (like we said, knitters are nice like that) or, if you're ready to invest, we suggest heading to your local yarn shop (a.k.a. LYS in knitter-speak).

If you're in the UK, Europe, or Australia, you'll be looking for 5-6mm needles and some 'aran' or 'chunky' weight yarn. They'll know what you're talking about. In the US, you'll ask for size 8-10 needles and 'worsted' to 'chunky' weight yarn. (Like imperial and metric measurement systems, there are still different conventions for sizing needles and yarn in different countries.) If you want to order supplies online, the same terms apply. And if you want our personal recommendation for great starter supplies, we love BC Garn Semilla Grosso yarn and straight, short wooden needles in size 6mm / US 10.

Once you've got some yarn and needles, you can get going! This part will take you through from casting on (making foundation loops), to the knit stitch, purl stitch, and casting off (fastening off your stitches so they don't unravel). These techniques are the building blocks of knitting and once you have practiced them you'll be ready for anything! Mainly for knitting, but just think about that extra boost you'll get from learning something new.

You will need:

(UK, EUROPE, AUSTRALIA)
5-6mm knitting needles
Aran or chunky weight yarn

(USA)
Size 8-10 knitting needles
Worsted to bulky weight yarn

CASTING ON

Before you can knit, you need to cast on. This means getting some foundation loops onto your needles so that you can begin to make stitches. Knitting is essentially loops caught within loops, so we need to start somewhere, right? Start by making a slip knot, as shown here.

How to Make a Slip Knot

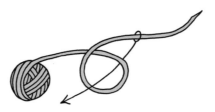

1. Arrange your yarn as if to make a knot, with a tail of around 15cm / 6".

2. Pull your loop through as shown, but do not pull it all the way through.

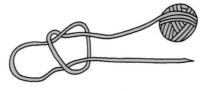

3. Your yarn should look like this.

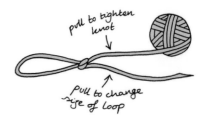

pull to tighten knot

pull to change size of loop

4. Now tighten the knot so that you have a loop as shown. If you pull the end that is attached to the yarn you can tighten the knot. Don't pull it too hard! You want the knot to be snug but not too tight. If you pull the loose end you can change the size of the loop.

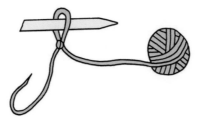

5. You can now place your loop on your knitting needle... and it becomes your very first stitch! Make sure it's sitting on the needle as shown, with its left leg behind the needle and right leg in front.

How to Cast On

There are almost as many ways to cast on as there are knitters, here we show you how to do the Knitted Cast-On.

1. Make a slip knot and place on needle. This is your first stitch. Hold this needle in your left hand.

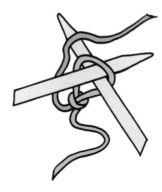

2. Hold your empty needle in your right hand. Insert right-hand needle into first stitch from front to back, as shown. Wrap yarn around tip of right-hand needle.

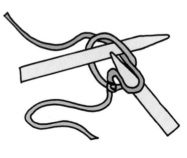

3. Use the tip of your right needle to pull the wrapped yarn through your first stitch.

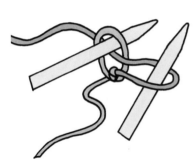

4. Pull loop all the way through by drawing your right-hand needle out of the stitch on your left-hand needle completely.

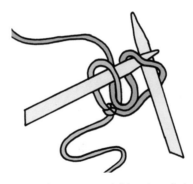

5. Place loop onto your left-hand needle by inserting the tip of your left-hand needle into the loop so that the left leg of the loop sits behind the needle and the right leg sits in front, as shown.

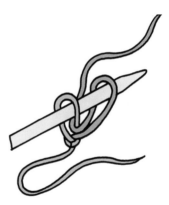

6. You now have two stitches!

7. Continue to cast on by inserting right-hand needle into the stitch closest to the tip of your left-hand needle, and wrap yarn over tip of right needle.

8. Pull loop of wrapped yarn through by drawing the right-hand needle out of the stitch and place on left-hand needle as in Step 5.

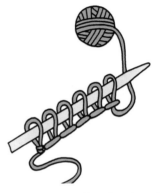

9. Repeat steps 7 and 8 until you have the required number of stitches.

THE KNIT STITCH

There are two major methods of holding your yarn when you are knitting. These are often referred to as English and Continental. Traditionally, most knitters in continental Europe use a method of knitting whereby they hold the yarn they are working with in their left hand. This method is also known as 'picking' because knitters quickly 'pick up' each stitch. Lydia, though British, taught herself to knit with videos online and just happened to choose this method.

In the UK, most knitters typically use the English style which consists of carrying your yarn in your right hand to make stitches. Meghan learned to knit in America, where there is a mix of knitters who use the English and Continental methods. It usually depends on your teacher and their knitting ancestors. For example, a knitter might have had a German grandmother who taught them how to knit - hence they knit Continental or 'pick'. In Meghan's case, she learned from someone who happened to knit in the English style, so that's how she's knit ever since. The English method is also sometimes called 'throwing' because of the way you wrap the yarn around the needle.

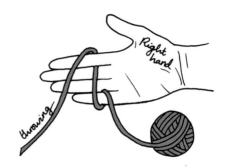

Before you pick up your needles, it's a good idea to hold your yarn securely. There are many ways to do this, but here are our suggested ways. You might adjust this slightly to suit you, or find a new way entirely! We aren't judging! If you decide to 'pick' your yarn you will hold it in your left hand, and if you 'throw' it you will hold it in your right.

How to Knit - Picking

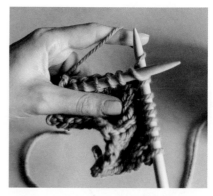

1. Hold the needle with your cast-on stitches in your left hand. With yarn held in back, drape the yarn over the index finger of your left hand and use your other fingers to support the needle and trap the strand of yarn. Insert your right-hand needle into the stitch on the left-hand side. Direct the right-hand needle through the loop and out the other side as shown. Make sure your needles cross diagonally.

2. Manoeuvre your index finger to wrap the yarn over the tip of your right-hand needle, making a little bridge of yarn over it that runs from left to right. This loop of wrapped yarn is the start of a new stitch!

3. Draw this wrapped yarn through by reversing your right-hand needle out the stitch and bringing the loop with it.

How to Knit - Throwing

1. Hold the needle with your cast-on stitches in your left hand. Keeping the working yarn held in back (behind your right-hand needle) insert your right-hand needle into the stitch on the left-hand needle by entering from the left-hand side. Direct the right-hand needle through the loop and out the other side as shown. Make sure your needles cross diagonally.

3. Draw this wrapped yarn through by reversing your right-hand needle out the stitch and bringing the loop with it.

4. Use your right-hand needle to slide the stitch on your left-hand needle to the tip and allow it to drop off the end. You've just knit one stitch!

2. Use your right hand to pick up your yarn and wrap it over the tip of your right-hand needle, making a little bridge of yarn over it that runs from left to right. This loop of wrapped yarn is the start of a new stitch!

4. Use your right-hand needle to slide the stitch on your left-hand needle to the tip and allow it to drop off the end. You've just knit one stitch!

There is no right or wrong way to knit as long as the end result comes out OK! There are advantages to both methods, so we'd recommend trying out both and seeing what feels more comfortable to you. If you ever learned to knit as a small child, you may find that one method comes to you more easily than the other.

Top Tip! Yarn in Front or Back

When we reference holding your yarn 'in back', it hangs on the side of the needles away from you. When your yarn is held 'in front', it hangs on the side of the needles nearest you.

There is a popular little poem that is often used to help people of all ages remember the basic steps of the knit stitch:

> **In through the front door,**
> **Run around the back,**
> **Hop through the window,**
> **Off jumps Jack.**

In simpler terms, you might think to yourself, 'In, around, through, off'. Either way, repeating these phrases to yourself with each stitch will help you to ensure you haven't missed a step and also help you get a little rhythm going.

Here's a visual guide to what your yarn and needles will be doing when working knit stitches.

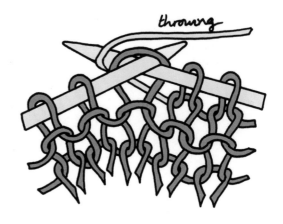

2.1. If throwing, use your right hand to wrap the yarn over tip of right-hand needle.

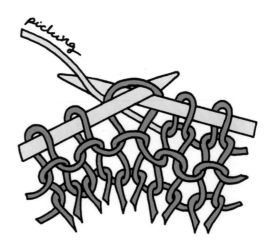

2.2. If picking, use your right-hand needle to 'pick' the yarn held in left hand to wrap around right-hand needle.

How to Make a Knit Stitch

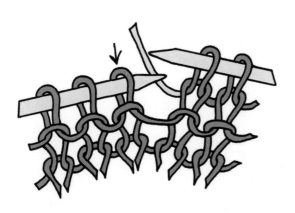

1. Ensure your yarn is held at the back of work. Insert right-hand needle into stitch on left-hand needle by entering from left-hand side of stitch and through the loop.

3. Pull loop of wrapped yarn through by drawing the right-hand needle out of the stitch.

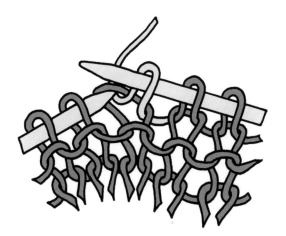

4. Use right-hand needle to guide stitch off left-hand needle.

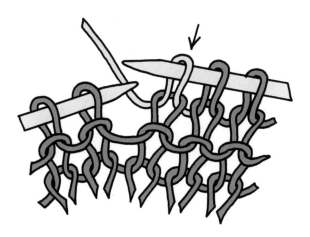

5. You've just knit one stitch!

To practise and really make sure you've got the hang of it, we recommend that you cast on around 20 stitches and knit every stitch until you reach the end of the row. Suddenly all your stitches will have magically travelled from your left needle to your right! Then you simply put the needle with all the stitches back in your left hand, the empty needle in your right hand, and continue. Keep on going until you really feel confident about the knit stitch. Warning: this may take some time. Don't worry, just set yourself up with your favourite album or podcast, and maybe a cup of tea, and enjoy not looking at a screen for a while!

Help! I have more stitches than I started with!
You may find that you end up with more stitches than you started with, and that's OK. Once you've built up some practice time, you'll get better and that will stop happening. You can avoid one common mistake that adds stitches by inspecting the first stitch of every row. Make sure that the yarn is hanging to the front of your knitting rather than flipped backwards. When it's flipped backwards it can look like two stitches instead of one, which will of course increase the number of stitches you have on every row!

Correct: How the first stitch in row should look.

Incorrect: How the first stitch in row should not look.

Help! My first stitch is too loose!
Keep in mind that the first stitch of every row might look and feel a little loose to you. This is OK, and nothing to worry about. You'll find this will even out the more you practise your knitting. For now, it's no problemo.

THE PURL STITCH

Now that you're a knit stitch pro, you can move on to purling!
A purl is a kind of reverse knit stitch (in Spanish, 'purl' is 'reverso', which just means 'reverse'). A purl stitch looks just like a knit stitch from the back, and vice-versa. Once again, there are two methods, depending on whether you throw or pick.

How to Purl - Picking

1. Hold your needle with your stitches ready to be purled in your left hand and your working needle in the right. With yarn held in front, loop the yarn over the index finger of your left hand.

2. Manoeuvre your index finger to wrap the yarn over the tip of your right-hand needle, making a little bridge of yarn over it that runs around the back from right to left.

3. Guide your right-hand needle out of the stitch you just entered, drawing the loop of wrapped yarn with it, so this loop now sits on your right-hand needle.

4. Use your right-hand needle to slide the stitch on your left-hand needle to the tip and allow it to drop off the end. You've just purled a stitch!

How to Purl - Throwing

1. Hold your needles with your stitches ready to be purled in your left hand and your yarn and working needle held in the right. With yarn held in front, insert your right-hand needle through the front of the stitch on your left-hand needle.

2. Use your right hand to wrap the yarn around the back of the tip of the right-hand needle.

3. Guide your right-hand needle under the stitch you just entered, drawing the loop of wrapped stitch with it.

4. This loop now sits on your right-hand needle.

5. Use your right-hand needle to slide the stitch on your left-hand needle to the tip and allow it to drop off the end.

6. You've just purled a stitch and are ready to repeat!

We like the poem for purling even better than the one for the knit stitch:

> **In through the back,**
> **Round the front,**
> **Out the back door,**
> **Jack must be drunk.**

If you've still got your stitches on your needles from practising your knit stitch, you can just start a new row with purls instead. After you've worked a few rows, you may notice that purl stitches look just like knit stitches when you look at them from the other side. And you would be right. When worked alone, rows and rows of knit stitches look exactly like rows and rows of purl stitches. It's only when we combine the two that things start looking different. For now, keep on purlin' on until you're a purl pro. Here's a visual guide to what your yarn and needles will be doing when working purl stitches.

How to Make a Purl Stitch

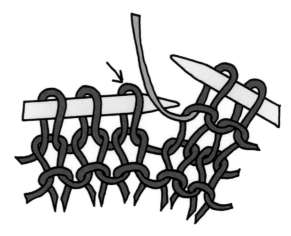

1. Ensure working yarn is at front of work. Insert right-hand needle into front of stitch from right to left.

2.1. If picking, use left hand to loop yarn over tip of right-hand needle.

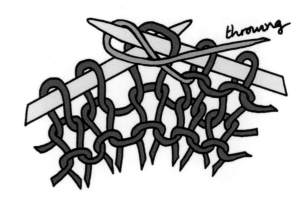

2.2. If throwing, use right hand to wrap yarn around tip of right-hand needle as shown.

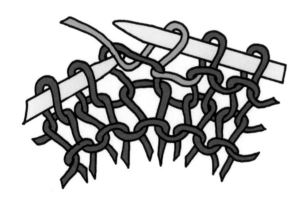

Top Tip! Reading Your Knitting

To help distinguish your knits from your purls, think of the purl stitch as being horizontal, like a pearl necklace, and a knit stitch as vertical, wrapping around like a knitted scarf.

3. Pull loop of wrapped yarn through by drawing the right-hand needle out of the stitch.

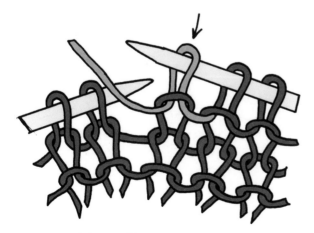

4. Use right-hand needle to guide stitch off left-hand needle.

5. You've just purled one stitch!

1.3

CASTING OFF

When it is time for your knitting to come off the needles, you need to secure each stitch so that it can't unravel. In the UK and many other English-speaking countries, this process is known as 'casting off' whereas, in the US, it is referred to as 'binding off'. As they say, Britain and America are two countries divided by a common language!

This is the most commonly used method for casting off, though you'll find that as you become more advanced, other techniques can be used to achieve different effects.

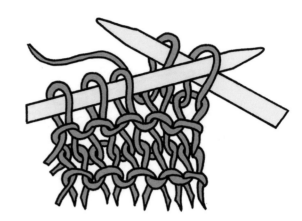

3. Using left-hand needle, pick up first stitch worked on right-hand needle.

How to Cast Off

1. Start at the beginning of a new row.

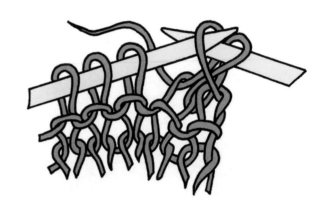

4. Lift and leap-frog the first stitch over the second stitch, making sure that second stitch remains on right-hand needle.

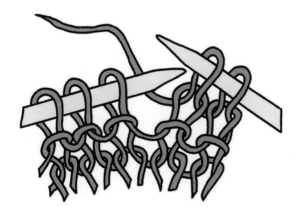

2. Knit two stitches.

5. Drop the lifted stitch off the end of right-hand needle and remove left-hand needle from the loop - one stitch cast off!

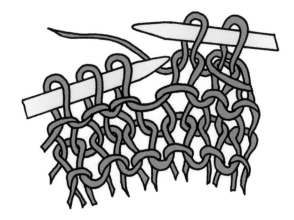

6. Knit one stitch - two stitches on right-hand needle.

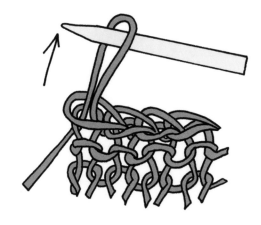

9. Use right-hand needle to draw the tail through.

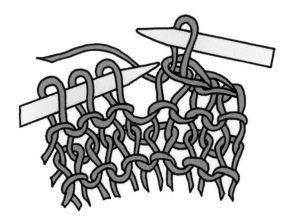

7. Repeat steps 3-6 until one stitch remains.

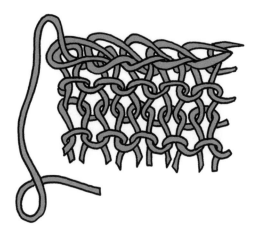

10. You have now cast off all your stitches! Time to weave in your tail, see page 27.

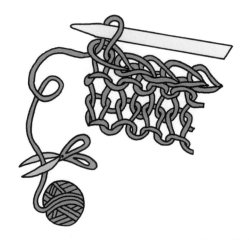

8. To finish casting off and secure knitting, cut yarn leaving a 20cm / 8" tail.

YOUR FIRST PROJECT: WARM UP

Squishy garter stitch coasters
(or blanket squares, or a future scarf, or...)

Now you're ready to knit some squidgy little squares! We're also going to try reading a pattern. Patterns may look intimidating, but fear not - it's no more complicated than writing LOL instead of 'laughing out loud'. So why not just k for 'knit' and p for 'purl'? How about just sts for 'stitches' or CO for 'cast on'? See? Not so intimidating after all. Let's give it a go!

k	Knit	**CO**	Cast on
p	Purl	**RS**	Right side of fabric
St(s)	Stitch(es)	**WS**	Wrong side of fabric

(p.s. There is a whole abbreviations list at the back of this book, so you can always refer to it if need be!).

Garter Stitch Coasters

Garter stitch is what we call knitting that is all one kind of stitch - either all knit, or all purl. It looks the same on both sides and is generally the easiest stitch pattern to do. It's deliciously spongy and always looks great - especially when it's not knit too loosely. Here are instructions for making these squares in either knit or purl so you can practise doing both.

These squares are like knitted building blocks. You can use them on their own as coasters, or sew them together to make a quilt or even a scarf! Here's a visual guide for how to sew your squishy squares together.

You Will Need:

Yarn: BC Garn Semilla Grosso (or 50g of aran / heavy worsted weight yarn)

Needles: 6mm / US 10 knitting needles

Notions: Tapestry needle
(also known as a darning needle)

Knitted Garter Stitch Square

CO 15 sts.
Row 1 (RS): K to end.
Row 2 (WS): K to end.

Rep Rows 1-2 12 more times.
Cast off all sts.

Purled Garter Stitch Square

CO 15 sts.
Row 1 (RS): P to end.
Row 2 (WS): P to end.

Rep Rows 1-2 12 more times.
Cast off all sts.

How to Sew Garter Stitch Squares Together Using Mattress Stitch

1. Thread a tapestry needle with your working yarn or a matching yarn (here we're using a contrast colour to make it clear). Insert your tapestry needle into the top knit bump of the first row.

2. On the opposite side of the seam, pick up the bottom knit bump on the corresponding row.

3. Weave back and forth to join the two sides together, passing your needle under the top knit bump on one side and then the bottom knit bump on the other, working your way up the rows.

4. As you continue up the rows, gently pull both ends of your yarn to close the seam at intervals, being careful not to pull too tight, and keeping the tension even. Marvel in the magic of mattress stitch and weave in ends to finish.

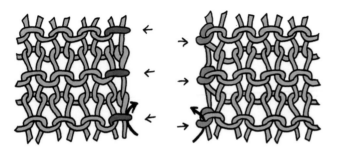

RS

When sewing your squares together use this guide to help you identify the top knit bump (shown in green) and bottom knit bump (shown in burgundy). The curved arrow shows the direction your yarn should travel through the bump.

FAQ!

Q: What's this about RS (right side) and WS (wrong side)?
A: Right side and wrong side refer to the side of your work that will face the world when you are finished knitting. The right side is the public-facing side (like the outside of a sweater) and the wrong side is the inside (like the inside of a sock). To be honest, it doesn't really matter with these little squares so don't get too worried about it just yet!

Q: How can I tell how many rows I have done?
A: That can be tricky, but with garter stitch, you will see little ridges appear. Each ridge is actually two rows worth of knitting.

Q: OK, I knit my square and cast off my stitches, now what?
A: Woo! Congratulations! Now you'll have the tails of your yarn from your cast-on and cast-off just hanging out. Let's move right along to our next section on weaving in yarn ends.

TIDYING UP: WEAVING IN YARN ENDS

You might be tempted to just cut the tails, or yarn ends, off your project once you're done. Eep! That could lead to your project unravelling and we don't want that.

You actually have to weave in the ends of your yarn so your stitches are nice and secure. There are about a zillion ways of doing this, but here's one of our go-to faves.

How to Weave in Ends

1. Thread your tapestry needle with the tail end. On the wrong side of your work, skim the tapestry needle diagonally through a few stitch bumps

2. Pull yarn through and point your needle to catch through the stitch bumps in the direction of the bottom edge of your knitting.

3. Repeat, skimming through a few stitches one more time.

4. Cut the tail close to your work, ensuring the woven tail is hidden from the right side of your work.

THE RIGHT STUFF
How to Choose Your Tools and Materials

What Colour?!

Guess what! You don't have to use the exact same yarn and needles as your pattern (or book!) calls for. In fact, the beauty and fun of knitting is that you can do it your way. The better you get at knitting, the more you can play around with your materials, but off the bat, the first place you can improvise is with colour. A yarn shop will become your artist's palette. It is totally OK to spend an hour (or hours) deliberating the perfect colour for a sweater. Equally, it is totally OK to picture the perfect colour in your head and then not stop until you've found the exact hand-dyed colour you've been dreaming of. It probably exists! (If not, you may go down a yarn-dyeing rabbit hole yourself. We won't judge.)

Which Yarn?!

You may also find that your local yarn shop (LYS) doesn't carry the exact yarn your pattern calls for. This is OK and not surprising. These days, there is an abundance of yarn brands, and this is to be celebrated. The fact that your pattern may have come from a designer online who lives in another country may also affect the availability of the yarn used. If you have a friendly, helpful LYS they should be happy to guide you through choosing an appropriate substitute yarn. We both used to work in an LYS and it was definitely part of our job to help customers in this way, so don't be shy!

If the shop is busy, or they are unable to help you, the best way to find a substitute for a yarn is to check how many metres per gram (or yards per ounce) there are in the ball of yarn (all this info will be on the yarn's label). We suggest BC Garn Semilla Grosso for our Garter Stitch Squares. It has 80 metres / 87 yards in a 50 gram ball. So if you find another yarn with a similar metreage or yardage per weight, you're golden! For example, a yarn that's 100 grams with 160 metres / 175 yards would work perfectly, because it has the same ratio of metres to grams.

What if I Don't Like Wool?!

Now let's talk about fibre. Wool is the beloved traditional knitting fibre and we absolutely recommend it for your first projects. There is a time and a place for acrylics, cottons, linens, and all the other fibres out there, but we're big wool fans for a few reasons. To start with, wool is a wonderful, natural resource; knitting is a tactile experience that can take you away from screens and technology, so we encourage you to feel all the feels. It's true that the softness of wool varies depending on the breed of the sheep and the ways in which it has been processed but we encourage you to explore the wools of the world. You may think it's itchy, but we are sure you can find a wool that feels great to you.

Secondly, wool has great elasticity. We've found that newbie knitters tend to work their stitches really tightly. This will ease up over time as you relax into things. But, to make it easier on yourself as you learn, choosing a nice bouncy wool will allow for some give in your knitting. Having said all this, we know that sometimes wool just isn't an option. In that case, there are some great cotton yarns that will work well for you while you are practising. Look for something around an aran or worsted weight that you can knit on 5mm / US 8 needles. If you need extra help choosing you can always ask at your local yarn shop and see what they recommend.

Which Needles?!

We recommend choosing some smooth wooden needles to get you started. Now that we're super-pro knitters, we really like metal circular needles (more on those later) to help us speed along. For new knitters, wooden needles help keep your yarn more secure as they are less slippery. Straight needles (as opposed to circulars) are great for beginners, as they keep things nice and simple.

WOUND RIGHT ROUND

Wrangling Skeins

Yarn comes in many forms off the shelf! Manufacturers and producers have different ways of packaging that are good to know about up-front.

1. Ball

With a ball, you're ready to knit pretty much as soon as you take the label off. You have a choice - knit with the end of the yarn that is on the outside of the ball, or dig into the middle and fish that end out. Option one is easier at the start, but option two will allow the ball to stay stationary as you knit.

2. Bullet

Bullets are pretty much the same as balls, just a little more... oblong? Same deal with pulling the end of the yarn from the outside or inside as above. Fun fact: sometimes when pulling the end of the yarn out of the inside of a ball or bullet, a clump of yarn will come out suddenly. This is what knitters refer to as yarn barf. It is the nicest barf you will ever see.

3. Skein

A skein is a large loop of yarn that has been twirled around itself to form a tidy twist. Skeins are also often referred to as hanks of yarn. Skeins generally should not be knit from as is; they need to be wound into a ball first, as demonstrated on the following page. You will most often see yarn in the form of a skein when it comes from a small producer, often an independent yarn dyer. Hand-dyed yarns, which are some of the most beautiful, unique, and special yarns out there, are typically dyed in an untwisted skein. Presenting the yarn in skein form means that knitters are able to see the variegations and subtleties that appear in hand-dyed yarns, in addition to the fact that skeins lay beautifully on the shelf in yarn shops or your home.

4. Cake

The ball that is produced when you use a ball winder is often called a cake. Some producers will sell their yarns already in the form of a cake. This is as useful and delicious as it sounds.

Skeins are wound into cakes using two lovely contraptions: a swift and a winder. They are used in tandem. The skein is stretched around the swift and then one end of the yarn is attached to the winder. The winder is either electric or powered with a hand-crank. Most local yarn shops will allow you to use their swift and winder or wind your yarn for you if you've bought it there.

Here is a swift and winder set up as you might see in your LYS. Note that there are different styles of swifts, but essentially they all work the same way, holding your skein in place while you wind it.

It's quick and easy to use a swift and winder (as you can see on the facing page), but it's also possible to wind your skein by hand. Just make sure to keep the skein taught while you wind from it. It's useful to have a buddy to help with this, or if your buddies are all off doing something else (they are missing out) you can place the skein around the back of a chair, or even around your knees.

Winding a Skein

1. Remove any labels from your skein and gently unwrap your yarn from a skein into a loop.

2. Lift your loop of yarn over and open the swift (like an umbrella) to meet the yarn and hold it in place. To keep skeins tidy and untangled, dyers tie the yarn at intervals. Carefully snip these knots. One of the knots will include both ends of the skein, which makes it very easy to find!

3. Take your end and thread it through the tension loops on your winder, then fix it into the groove on the top of the winder which will keep it in place. Steadily turn the handle of the winder to start transforming your skein into a cake!

4. Once your skein has transformed into a cake, gently pull it off of the winder. Tuck the end of your yarn into the outside of the cake and you're ready to knit. You might like to tuck the label into the centre of your cake to keep it safe for future reference.

DOING IT RIGHT
Swatching and Blocking

Those little Garter Stitch Squares we did before? Those are basically swatches. What do you think of when you see the word 'swatch'? Paint swatches? Fabric samples? Well, knitting swatches are essentially both. When you're about to embark on a project that needs to be a certain size, or to fit your body in some way, you'll want to do a test swatch. This means working up a small sample of knitting with the yarn and needles you intend to use for your project. You see, just like everyone has different handwriting, everyone also knits to a different tension. Some people knit more loosely or more tightly than others just because of the unique way they hold their yarn or needles. In fact, an individual might knit differently at different times in their life - you might find you knit more tightly when you're anxious, or more loosely when on vacation.

Every (good) knitting pattern will indicate the tension, or gauge, to which you should knit. As we said, this is especially important for items that need to fit. If you knit more loosely than the person who designed your pattern, your sweater or hat will be looser too, sometimes to comedic effect!

To ensure that your tension is the same as in the pattern, you've got to swatch. We can't tell you how many times we've heard of a knitter spending months on a project only to discover at the end that it doesn't fit (in fact, we've been guilty of this too). The best way to avoid this is to swatch, swatch, swatch. We'll say it again, SWATCH! Think of it as the warm-up before the big game - it'll be worth it!

How to Swatch

Step 1: Knit a Square

So how do you swatch anyway?! Check the gauge section of your pattern. It will say something like this: 15 sts and 20 rows = 10cm / 4" in garter stitch. This means that 15 stitches and 20 rows should come out as a 10cm / 4" square. In order to check your gauge (to see whether you get the same number of sts per 10cm square as the pattern designer did) you need to cast on more than the amount of stitches you need to measure. In this case, you will need to measure 15 sts so we would recommend casting on an even 20. This way it's easier to measure and you'll get a better feel for the texture of the fabric you will be making. Once you have cast on, knit in garter stitch (or whatever stitch pattern is indicated) for more than 20 rows. This should result in a jaunty little square, also known as a swatch!

Step 2: Block the Swatch

Now give the swatch a nice, soapy bath. This step is essential if you intend to wash your finished project (please say that you do...). Yarn is kind of like hair in the sense that it resets when you wash it. We usually hand wash all our knits, so do the same with your swatch. Get a little wool wash, or gentle shampoo, fill up a sink with warm (but not hot) water and then submerge the swatch. Let it soak for at least 15 minutes. When you take it out of the water, you can squeeze out the excess moisture, but try not to wring it. The less you agitate your precious swatch, the better. You can roll it up in a clean towel and press gently to squeeze more moisture out. This will speed up the drying time. Lay the swatch out flat on an out-of-the-way surface. Once it's dry, it's time to measure it.

This process is called blocking. You might notice that your swatch looks better post-blocking than it did before. Getting moisture running through all your new stitches relaxes the yarn. This sets the stitches in place and can even erase any unevenness that was there before. It's magic.

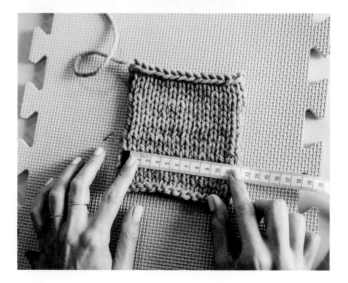

Step 3: Measure Up

To measure the swatch, lay it out on a completely flat surface (so... not your lap). Grab a ruler - we prefer a ruler to a measuring tape since it's rigid but if you use a tape measure keep an eye on it, and don't let it bend while you are measuring. You can even get a fancy gauge-measuring ruler (like we have used on the left) - they're rad. Now it's time to count how many stitches you have in a 10cm or 4" space. We do 4" instead of 1" so that there is enough space to get an accurate average per inch. Most knitting patterns will state the gauge over 10cm or 4" as well. You can use two pins to mark off the 4" length on the swatch and then count each stitch within that space, if you like. In garter stitch, each little curve is one stitch. In stocking stitch (or stockinette as it's also called) each stitch looks like a V on the front (or the "right side") of the fabric.

The knitter's jackpot is getting gauge on the first try. Sometimes it happens, sometimes not. If you don't have the same number of stitches that the pattern states right off the bat, don't worry: it's completely normal. It just means you need to swatch again. You don't need to move on to a different yarn necessarily, especially if you are using the yarn called for in the pattern or something close to it. What you will need to do change is your needle size. This can be frustrating for new knitters who don't already have an arsenal of needles (one day soon you will!). Needles determine how big the loops of yarn become. So small needles = small loops, and big needles = big loops. That's why thinner yarns are typically knit with smaller needles and vice versa.

So say you have more stitches in 4" than is called for in your pattern. That means your stitches are smaller than they need to be, because more of them can fit into that 4" space. What you need to do is try again with bigger needles. How much bigger depends on how big the discrepancy is between your gauge and the pattern's gauge, but usually one needle size up is a good place to start. If you don't have enough stitches in the 4" space, then you have fewer stitches than the pattern calls for and you need to go down a needle size. That will make your stitches smaller, and you'll be able to fit more into that 4" space. Then you swatch again. *Hopefully* second time's a charm, but if not, guess what - time to swatch again! We find it rare that a knitter will need to swatch more than three times, so don't let the swatching get you down. It. Will. Be. Worth. It. We *promise*.

Once you've got your stitch gauge on, check your row gauge too - i.e. how many rows of knitting fit into the 10cm / 4" space vertically. Ideally both your stitch gauge and your row gauge will be spot on, but if not, generally your stitch gauge is the more important to get right.

Joining New Yarn at the Start of a Row

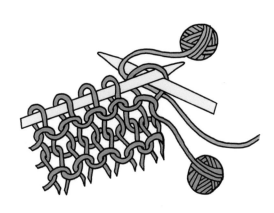

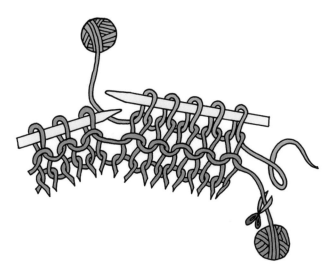

1. Pick up the 'new' yarn (shown in purple), ready to knit. Insert right-hand needle into first stitch to knit as normal but wrap with new yarn. Draw needle through to make a stitch, leaving a tail of at least 20cm / 8" of your new yarn.

2. Continue knitting with new yarn. Cut your old yarn (shown in yellow), leaving a tail of at least 20cm / 8". Weave in loose ends at end of project (see page 27).

THE PROJECTS

Welcome to Part 2! Now that you've got to grips with the nuts and bolts of knits and purls, it's time to embark upon creating your own custom-knit wardrobe. Here we have all manner of knits for you to make, from mitts and hats, to jumpers and socks! We have organised the projects in this order so that you can work through them from start to finish, picking up new techniques as you go! Don't be put off if several techniques are introduced in one project; you won't need to learn them simultaneously but as you work through you will build on your knitting knowledge. One of the great things about knitting is that you can always unravel it and start again. This might not sound very appealing at first but how many areas of life are this forgiving? Remember that learning involves making mistakes and at the end of this learning process you will have so many colourful and lovely things to show for the journey.

Of course we know that working through from project 1 to 10 might not be the best fit for everyone. So we have a list of which techniques are introduced with each project, so you can see at a glance which you would like to dive into!

Project 1: Ce - Fingerless Mitts
Treat your knitter's hands to the luxury of handmade mitts.

- How to recognise a knit or purl stitch
- Ribbing and stocking stitch
- Mattress Stitch

Pattern on page 40

Project 2: Mary / Bobby / Juju - Simple Cowls in Three Stitch Patterns
The neck's best thing to a scarf... a cowl!

- 2.1: Mary - Garter Stitch Cowl
- 2.2: Bobby - Moss Stitch Cowl
- 2.3: Juju - Broken Rib Cowl

Pattern on page 48

Introduction to Knitting in the Round
Be like The Beach Boys and get around!

- Working in the round: 40cm circular needles
- Using stitch markers
- Small circular knitting in the round: Magic Loop and DPNs

Project 3: Dan - Hat in the Round
Get ahead and knit a hat.

- Long-tail cast-on
- Making a pom pom
- Joining in a new colour
- Decreasing (k2tog and ssk)
- Threading yarn through stitches

Pattern on page 68

Project 4: John & Juliet - Cuffs in the Round
Coming round to cuffs.

- Slipping stitches

Pattern on page 80

Project 5: Fiona / Alice - Cabled Scarves
Textured twists for a classic scarf.

- 5.1: Fiona - Simple Cabled Scarf
- 5.2: Alice - Adventurous Cabled Scarf
- Cables
- Introduction to chart reading

Pattern on page 86

Project 6: Rosa - First Mittens in the Round
Magic mittens for frosty days.

- Increasing (M1L and M1R)
- Picking up stitches

Pattern on page 98

Project 7: Chris / James - First Jumpers
Time to jump(er) in with your first garment!

- 7.1: Chris - First Jumper
- 7.2: James - Waffle Jumper
- Three-needle cast-off
- Picking up stitches

Pattern on page 106

Project 8: Madeline - Simple Lace Cowl
How to get ace at lace.

- Yarn overs
- Blocking lace

Pattern on page 118

Project 9: Frankie - First Cardigan
Oh this? Just a cardigan that I made!

- Knitting flat on circular needles
- Backwards loop cast-on

Pattern on page 124

Project 10: Rachel - Simple Bed Socks
Make sure you're cosy from head to toe.

- Turning heels and short rows
- Grafting (aka Kitchener stitch)
- Decreasing (p2tog)
- Measuring feet for socks

Pattern on page 134

Project 1

C–E

Fingerless Mitts

You can cast on. You can knit. You can purl. We believe in you. YOU CAN MAKE THESE MITTS. While making them, you are going to put those knits and purls to use AND you are going to mix the two stitches together to create different stitch patterns! The cuffs of the mitts are worked in 1x1 rib - which is the alternating of knit and purl stitches in the same row. The rest of the mitt is worked in stocking stitch (also called stockinette), wherein one row is knit and the next row is purled to create a pleasingly flat fabric on one side. In a beautiful semi-solid, hand-dyed yarn, these mitts are addictive to make. We suggest a pair for every member of your family this gift-giving season.

Notes on Construction:
The mitts are knit from the bottom cuff up to the top of the opening for your fingers. Each mitt is worked in one flat piece which is folded in half and seamed, leaving an opening for the thumb hole.

Techniques You Need to Know:
- Casting on (see page 12)
- Knit stitch (see page 14)
- Purl stitch (see page 18)
- Casting off (see page 22)

Techniques Introduced:
- Recognising a knit stitch vs. a purl stitch
- Ribbing
- Stocking stitch
- Mattress stitch on stocking stitch

1x1 Rib

Stocking Stitch

Top Tip! Parentheses & Brackets

Most patterns include multiple sizes, providing different instructions for each size. Sizes are organised in a parenthetical list and instructions follow the same sequence throughout. So if we knit size 2 of our mitts from the size list 1 (2, 3), we follow the second number throughout and cast on 41 stitches when instructed to cast on 37 (41, 45) stitches. Be sure to distinguish stitch counts in parentheses from repeating stitches in brackets, which all sizes follow - e.g. [k1, p1] in the cuff.

All About Abbreviations

For your first pattern, we thought we'd give you a leg-up with the abbreviations used. For future patterns, all abbreviations are listed in the back of this book for easy reference!

St(s)	Stitch(es)
St st	Stocking stitch
k	Knit
p	Purl
rep	Repeat
RS	Right side of fabric
WS	Wrong side of fabric

Sizes: 1 (2, 3)

Finished circumference at widest point: 17.5 (19, 21.5) cm /
7 (7½, 8½)"

Finished length: 19 cm / 7½"

Yarn: The Uncommon Thread Merino DK (DK/light worsted
weight; 100% Merino wool; 229 m / 250 yds per 100 g skein)

Shade: Fe203 (orange); 1 skein

OR Attic Room (brown); 1 skein

OR Space Oddity (blue); 1 skein

Size 1 - Fe203

Size 2 - Attic Room

Size 3 - Space Oddity

Gauge: 20 sts & 30 rows = 10 cm / 4" over stocking stitch
on 4 mm needles after blocking.

Needles: 4 mm / US 6 knitting needles

4.5 mm / US 7 knitting needles for cast-off (optional)

Always use a needle size that will result in the correct
gauge after blocking.

Notions: Tapestry needle

PATTERN BEGINS

(make 2 alike)

CUFF

Leaving a long tail of at least 15 cm / 6", using the knitted
cast-on method, cast on 37 (41, 45) sts.

Row 1 (RS): [K1, p1] to last st, k1.

Row 2 (WS): [P1, k1] to last st, p1.

Rep rows 1 and 2 until Cuff measures 8 cm / 3" from
cast-on edge, ending after a WS row (row 2).

HAND

Continue by working in St st as follows:

Row 1 (RS): Knit.

Row 2 (WS): Purl.

Rep rows 1 and 2 until mitt measures 16.5 cm / 6½" from
cast-on edge, ending after a WS row (row 2).

Continue in 1x1 Rib as follows:

Row 1 (RS): [K1, p1] to last st, k1.

Row 2 (WS): [P1, k1] to last st, p1.

Rep rows 1 and 2 for 2.5 cm / 1" until mitt measures 19 cm /
7½" from cast-on edge, ending after a WS row (row 2).
Cast off quite loosely in 1x1 Rib pattern (if desired, use a
larger needle to achieve a flexible edge).

FINISHING

Block mitts by allowing them to soak for at least 15 minutes
in lukewarm water. Remove from water, squeezing gently
to remove excess water. Lay flat to dry, pinning the edges
flat if necessary. Once completely dry, seam the two side
edges together with mattress stitch as follows: using the
long cast-on tail, seam from the bottom upwards for 10 cm
/ 4". Leave a gap of 5 cm / 2" for the thumbhole, then, using
a new length of yarn, begin seaming again to top of mitt.
Weave in ends and block to measurements.

a. Finished circumference at widest point: 17.5 (19, 21.5) cm
/ 7 (7½, 8½)"

b. Finished length: 19 cm / 7½"

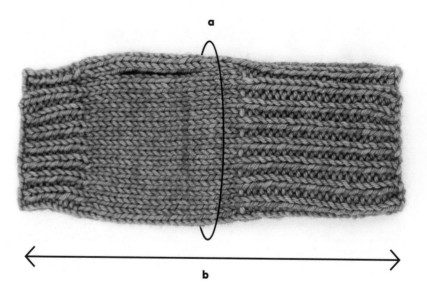

Recognising Stitches

Knitters often need to know whether they are working on the right or the wrong side of their fabric (see page 26 for a reminder). You can ensure you are on the correct side by learning to recognise stitches by sight; knitters call this reading your knitting.

Knit Stitch

A knit stitch will look like the letter 'V'. Imagine the loops on your needle are the heads of little people and each one is wearing a scarf over their shoulders with the ends dangling over their chest. This is what you should see when you have worked a knit stitch.

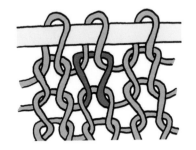

Purl Stitch

A purl stitch will look like a bump just under the stitch on your needle. You might like to think of this as a pearl (purl!) necklace sat around the neck of this stitch to help you remember.

Twisted Stitch

A twisted stitch is not the end of the world, but it will make your knitting look, well, twisted! Think of the two sides of the loop that sit on your needle as a pair of legs running towards the tip of your needle. In the first stitch, the front leg is stepping forward first in the race (which is the correct position). For the second stitch, the leg that is leaning forward is the back leg, making this is a twisted stitch. You may notice when you come to knit this stitch that is it not as easy to enter the loop, so check if it's twisted. (Need to fix a twisted stitch? See how on page 145).

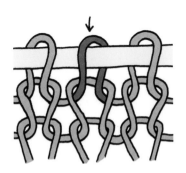

Ribbing

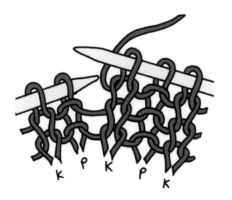

1. Here the last stitch on the right-hand needle has been knit, and the next stitch should be purled. The yarn is 'in back' meaning it's behind the needles, as this is the correct position for the working yarn for knit stitches.

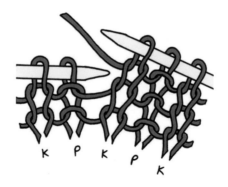

2. To get ready to purl you need your working yarn to be in front of your needles, on the side facing you. To move your working yarn from back to front pass it between the needles, as shown.

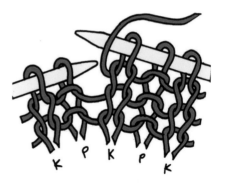

3. The working yarn is now at the front of the work. You are ready to purl!

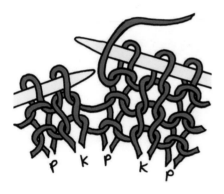

4. Here the last stitch on the right-hand needle was purled, and the next stitch should be knit. The yarn is 'in front', as this is the correct position for the working yarn for purl stitches.

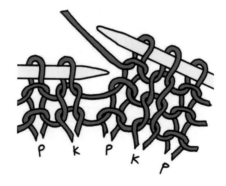

5. To get ready to knit the next stitch you need your working yarn to be behind (in back) of your needles, on the far side from you. To move your working yarn from front to back pass it between your needles, as shown.

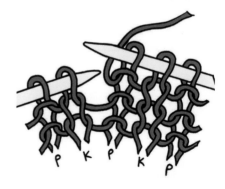

6. You are now ready to knit the next stitch. As you continue to work your ribbing you will pass your yarn from back to front to purl and front to back to knit.

Mattress Stitch on Stocking Stitch

If you gently pull your knitting width-wise, you'll see little horizontal bars of yarn, like rungs of a ladder, that run behind these stitches. You'll be picking these up when you seam.

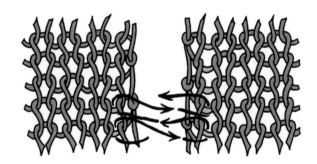

1. Thread a tapestry needle with your working yarn or a matching yarn (here, we're using a contrast colour to make it clear). Arrange your knitting so right sides are facing up. Insert your tapestry needle into the horizontal bar between the first and second stitches.

2. On the opposite side of the seam, insert your tapestry needle under the corresponding horizontal bar.

3. Weave back and forth to join the two sides together, passing your tapestry needle under the next rung of the ladder in between the stitches.

4. Gently pull both ends of your yarn to close the seam.

5. Just like magic, the seam is invisible! Repeat step 3 weaving back and forth, taking the time every couple of stitches to pull your yarn ends to close the seam. To finish, weave in ends.

Pattern 2.1: Mary
- Garter Stitch Cowl

Pattern 2.2: Bobby
- Moss Stitch Cowl

Pattern 2.3: Juju
- Broken Rib Cowl

M·A·R·Y

–

B·O·B·B·Y

–

J·U·J·U

Simple Cowls in Three Stitch Patterns

Cowls are much like a scarf but shorter, joined into a loop, and quicker to make. These three cowls are all the same length and will achieve the same purpose (cosiness), but each showcases a different stitch pattern. You can choose between trusty garter stitch (the same squidgy stitch used for the coasters from part 1), moss stitch (one of our faves), and a slightly fancier broken rib. All these stitch patterns are great ways to get more acquainted with the various ways knit and purl stitches can combine to create different textures. If you are so inclined then making all three wouldn't be a bad idea. But, of course, you can always just choose a fave and make that one!

Notes on Construction:
These cowls are made by knitting a rectangle of fabric which is then seamed to create a loop. The two short ends of the rectangle (the cast-on and cast-off ends) are the ones that are seamed.

Techniques You Need to Know:
  - Casting on (see page 12)
  - Knit stitch (see page 14)
  - Purl stitch (see page 18)
  - Casting off (see page 22)
  - Mattress stitch (see page 25)

Techniques Introduced:
  - Moss stitch
  - Broken rib
  - Casting off in pattern

Bonus Info:
Like so many things in knitting, the stitch patterns are better understood by doing than explaining. Even if you don't go ahead and make whole cowls, it's worth making a swatch of each!

What is moss stitch and is it like moss?
Well it definitely doesn't have to be green! Moss stitch, also known as seed stitch in the US, is created by staggering single rows of k1, p1. Each row has the same sequence as it would for a 1x1 rib (as seen in project 1), but rather than stacking columns of knits on top of each other and purls in the same way, each column alternates between the two like a chequerboard.

Broken rib? Sounds painful!
Broken rib is a combination of rib and moss stitch, with stacked columns of knits and purls separated by columns of alternating knits and purls. So the name just refers to the fact that the columns of knit and purl stitches are broken up by a different texture.

Top Tip! Casting Off in Pattern

In this pattern we ask you to 'cast off in pattern'. This means that rather than knitting each stitch before passing them over to fasten off, you knit or purl them as appropriate.

Moss Stitch

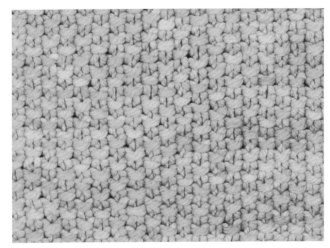

Broken Rib

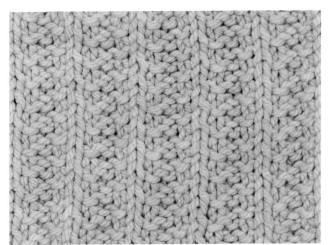

Garter Stitch

Pattern 2.1: Mary
- Garter Stitch Cowl

One size: 21 cm / 8½" deep x 92 cm / 36" circumference
Yarn: Malabrigo Chunky (chunky weight; 100% Merino wool; 95 m / 100 yds per 100 g skein)
Shade: CH094 Bergamota; 2 skeins
Gauge: 12 sts & 24 rows = 10cm / 4" over garter stitch on 8 mm needles after blocking.
Needles: 8 mm / US 11 knitting needles
Always use a needle size that will result in the correct gauge after blocking.
Notions: Tapestry needle

PATTERN BEGINS
Using the knitted cast-on method, cast on 26 sts.

Row 1: Knit.
Rep row 1 until piece measures 92 cm / 36" (or desired length) from cast-on edge, ensuring you have enough yarn remaining to cast off with – you will need a length of yarn at least three times the width of the piece.
Cast off.

FINISHING
Seam the short ends of the cowl together using mattress stitch.
Weave in ends and block to measurements.

a. Depth: 21 cm / 8½"
b. Circumference: 92 cm / 36"

Pattern 2.2: Bobby
- Moss Stitch Cowl

One size: 21 cm / 8½" deep x 92 cm / 36" circumference
Yarn: Malabrigo Chunky (chunky weight; 100% Merino wool; 95 m / 100 yds per 100 g skein)
Shade: CH021 Cactus Flower; 2 skeins
Gauge: 13 sts & 20 rows = 10cm / 4" over moss stitch on 8 mm needles after blocking.
Needles: 8 mm / US 11 knitting needles
Always use a needle size that will result in the correct gauge after blocking.
Notions: Tapestry needle

PATTERN BEGINS
Using the knitted cast-on method, cast on 27 sts.

Row 1: [K1, p1] to last st, k1.
Rep row 1 to form moss stitch (a knit stitch on top of a purl stitch and a purl on top of a knit) until piece measures 92 cm / 36" (or desired length) from cast-on edge, ensuring you have enough yarn remaining to cast off with – you will need a length of yarn at least three times the width of the piece.
Cast off in [k1, p1] rib pattern.

FINISHING
Seam the short ends of the cowl together using mattress stitch.
Weave in ends and block to measurements.

a. Depth: 21 cm / 8½"
b. Circumference: 92 cm / 36"

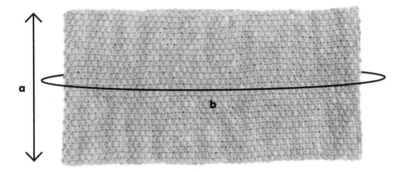

Pattern 2.3: Juju
- Broken Rib Cowl

One size: 17.5 cm / 7" deep x 92 cm / 36" circumference
Yarn: Malabrigo Chunky (chunky weight; 100% Merino wool;
95 m / 100 yds per 100 g skein)
Shade: CH083 Water Green; 2 skeins
Gauge: 16 sts & 20 rows = 10cm / 4" over broken rib on
8 mm needles after blocking.
Needles: 8 mm / US 11 knitting needles
Always use a needle size that will result in the correct
gauge after blocking.
Notions: Tapestry needle

PATTERN BEGINS
Using the knitted cast-on method, cast on 27 sts.

Row 1: [K2, p2] to last 3 sts, k2, p1.
Rep row 1 until piece measures 92 cm / 36" (or desired
length) from cast-on edge, ensuring you have enough
yarn remaining to cast off with – you will need a length
of yarn at least three times the width of the piece.
Cast off in [k2, p2] rib.

FINISHING
Seam the short ends of the cowl together using
mattress stitch.
Weave in ends and block to measurements.

a. Depth: 17.5 cm / 7"
b. Circumference: 92 cm / 36"

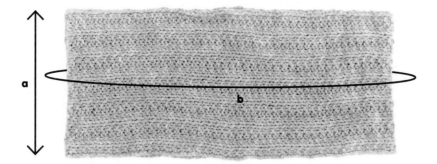

INTRODUCTION TO KNITTING IN THE ROUND

Knitting in the round, or circular knitting, opens up a whole new world to knitters. Instead of going back and forth in rows, you work in rounds to create a spiral that grows into a tube of knitting. Lots of items you will want to knit, for example hats, mitts, sleeves, socks, even some jumpers (a.k.a sweaters) are nothing but slightly modified tubes, so it's handy to be able to create tubes of fabric without seams.

There are three ways to knit in the round. You can use circular needles, which are simply needle tips attached to each other with a cord. The cord comes in various lengths, which you can choose depending on what you are going to make. Once you've cast on the correct number of stitches, you bend the cord to join the last stitch you cast on to the first stitch. This leaves them sitting next to each other to make a circle out of the stitches on your needles. You'll see what we're talking about on page 61. For smaller circumferences, you'll need to use double-pointed needles (page 64), or a long circular needle and a technique called 'Magic Loop' (page 66). Sounds fun, right? We recommend trying out each technique with some spare yarn before you dive into your project. This will help you decide which method you prefer and get comfortable using it.

Knitting in the round is a fundamental skill you'll return to again and again and it's very satisfying once you get the hang of it. Your knitting grows quickly and there are fewer seams to sew up when you're done, so you can wear your handknit sooner! Aside from being quick, seamless knitting is slinky, comfortable, and flows over the body. Seams can rub unpleasantly in some garments (like socks!) or interfere with complex colour patterns. Now don't get us wrong; we aren't saying seams should be banned! Seams can create tailoring and structure so definitely have their place. But the more ways you have to create fabric, the better stocked your toolbox will be and the more possibilities you have. We love knitting in the round and we hope you do, too!

Let's talk more about the three different ways to knit in the round: circular needles, double-pointed needles, and Magic Loop. The method you choose will depend first on the circumference of the thing you want to knit. Think about the difference in circumference of the body of a sweater versus the cuff of a mitten. It's a big difference! Anything with a circumference larger than 40cm/16" can be made with a circular needle. For smaller circumferences, you'll need to use double-pointed needles or the Magic Loop technique, whichever you prefer. This is because the tips of shorter circular needles can't bend around small pieces of knitting!

The easiest way to get started with knitting in the round is with a pair of 40cm/16" circular needles, which just so happens to be the correct length (or circumference once you're knitting in the round) to make a hat!

Here we have two tutorials: a quick drawing to show you how joining to work in the round happens, and a photo tutorial to show more detail.

How to Join to work in the Round

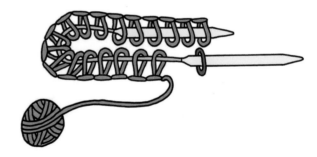

1. Cast on and ensure your stitches are not twisted. To mark the beginning of your round, place stitch marker on right needle.

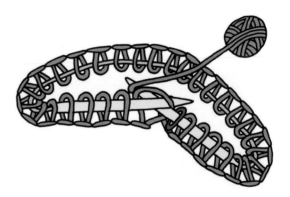

2. The first stitch of the round will be the first cast-on stitch. Manoeuvre your needles so your needle with the working yarn is the right-hand needle, and insert into first stitch to knit.

How to Join in the Round

1. Cast on your required number of stitches. It's important to make sure that your stitches are not twisted. In the photo above the sittches are sitting correctly.

Note: This is what you **do not** want! The cast-on has spiralled around the knitting needle cord, making 'twisted stitches'. Rectify this by rearranging the stitches so the cast-on is a neat line, as shown in Step 1.

2. In your right hand, place the needle which holds your last cast-on stitch (with your working yarn attached to it). Place a stitch marker on your right-hand needle.

3. Begin the round by knitting the first stitch on your left needle by inserting your right needle.

4. Wrap the right needle with your working yarn, draw this loop through and guide the stitch off your left-hand needle. That's knitting in the round!

5. Continue by knitting each stitch. Here you can see we've now knit two stitches. You'll work round the circle. When you get to your stitch marker, simply pass this from one needle to the other.

You'll have seen above that the last stitch you cast on is now cosied up to the first stitch you cast on and your stitches are in a circle. As you work in the round you won't ever need to turn your knitting as you did with straight needles; the right side of the work will always be facing you. This means that to achieve stocking stitch in circular knitting, you only ever have to do the knit stitch! Conversely, if you want to do garter stitch, you will have to alternate knit and purl rounds.

You may have noticed how we used a stitch marker to signal the beginning and end of a round. Because you are now working in a spiral, it's much harder to see where one row ends and the next begins without some kind of indicator. Stitch markers are handy tools that can be used for other things too, like marking where to make increases or decreases. If you don't have stitch markers, you can always make one by knotting a small piece of contrasting yarn into a loop.

You'll know when to put a marker on your needle because your pattern will say 'PM' meaning 'place marker'.

Using Stitch Markers

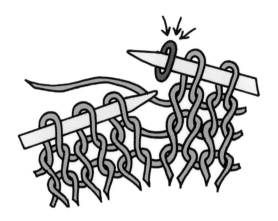

1. Stitch markers sit on your needle in between stitches. Place them on your needle as shown.

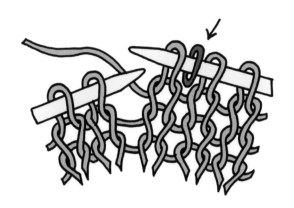

2. Here is a stitch marker in between two stitches.

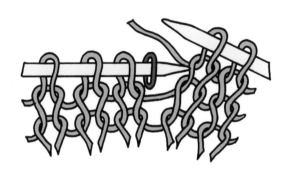

3. When you reach a marker...

4. Simply slip it from your left to right needle and carry on knitting or purling!

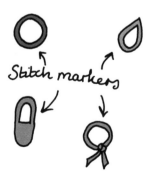

5. Here are some examples of stitch markers.

When it comes to knitting small circumferences, you have two choices: double-pointed needles or the Magic Loop technique. Regular circular needles won't cut it once your circumference falls below 40cm /16" because the small number of stitches needed won't stretch around the length of a circular needle.

The method you choose is entirely up to you! The end result is the same and it's only a question of which one you find easier. We list below the pros and cons of each technique so you can make an informed decision.

Double-Pointed Needles

Double-pointed needles, or DPNs, are sets of 4-5 needles that, you guessed it, are pointed at both ends. You cast your stitches onto one DPN and redistribute them over 3-4 needles, depending on your pattern. You then use a spare DPN to knit into these stitches (see adjacent tutorial).

Pros: DPNs are the more traditional tool and some patterns are written with them in mind, especially if you try knitting vintage patterns.

Cons: There are 4-5 small needles in a set and it's easy to misplace a needle over time. Some people find having to juggle 4-5 needles at one time very fiddly. There is also a higher likelihood of 'laddering', which means a small but visible gap that can appear where the needles meet. Tightening your stitches at these locations will minimise laddering.

How to Knit a Small Circumference in the Round Using Double-Pointed Needles (aka DPNs)

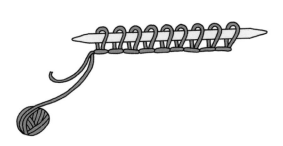

1. Cast on required number of stitches onto one DPN.

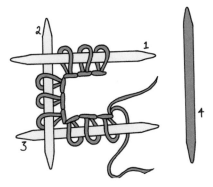

2. Redistribute stitches evenly over three DPNs by sliding purlwise, one at a time, onto needles. Arrange trio of DPNs as 3 sides of a square, with last cast-on stitch in the bottom right-hand corner on DPN 3. Make sure stitches are not twisted. 4th needle is ready for action!

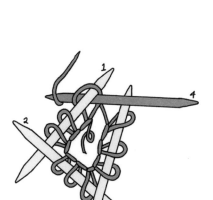

3. Bring tips of DPN 3 and 1 together to form a triangle. Insert DPN into first stitch on DPN 1 and knit this stitch. Knit across all stitches on DPN 1. DPN 4 now holds stitches and DPN 1 is empty.

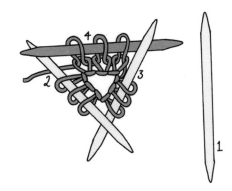

4. Now use DPN 1 to knit across stitches on DPN 2.

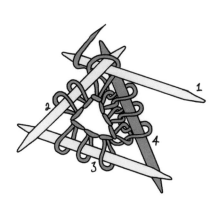

5. Continue knitting across each of the three DPNS in turn.

6. After a few rows, your knitting will look like this. It gets easier to work with DPNs when there's more fabric to anchor them, so your hard work will pay off!

Knitting in the Round Using Magic Loop
(Suitable for Both Small and Large Circumferences)

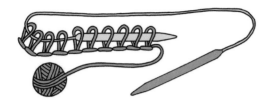

1. Cast on required number of stitches.

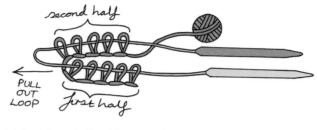

2. Split stitches in half and draw cord of circular needles out, creating a loop in the middle of stitches. Arrange two halves of stitches with working yarn on the second half/back needle. Be careful not to twist stitches.

3. Pull back needle so stitches slide onto cord and manoeuvre needle into position to work with front needle.

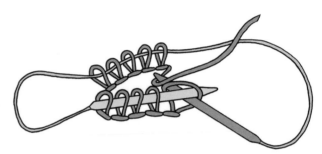

4. Knit first stitch, drawing working yarn from back needle. Pull yarn snug to avoid leaving a gap.

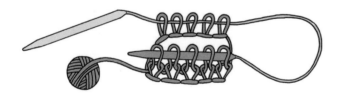

5. Knit to end.

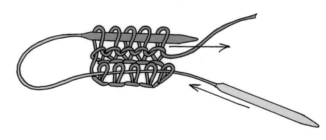

6. Turn work 180 degrees clockwise. Rearrange needles by first drawing front needle back and sliding stitches from cord onto needle. Then draw out back needle, allowing stitches just worked to slide onto cable.

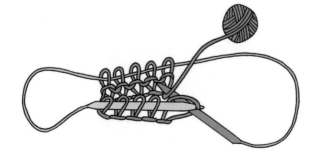

7. Knit your first stitch as shown. Pay attention to where your working yarn is; make sure it isn't looped around the cable of the circular needle or under the needle, which will create a gap. Knit all stitches to end. One round has now been worked.

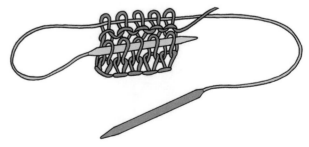

8. Repeat steps 6-7 to continue knitting in the round.

Magic Loop

Magic Loop is done with one very long circular needle (at least 80cm/32" in length). To create the smaller circumference, the extra length of the needle's cord is pulled out at two points to make a bunny-ear shape, leaving you with just the length you need in the middle for your knitting.

Pros: We find that long circular needles are more versatile than DPNs. They can be used for knitting flat, in the round, and at small or large circumferences. Using long circulars for Magic Loop also means that you won't ever find yourself struggling to look for that 4th needle as you might with DPNs.

Cons: Some people find having to rearrange their needles every round tedious. We find the process flows quickly once you get the hang of it.

Now you are armed with new techniques to can tackle the next project, which is knit in the round. So, round you go!

Project 3

D-A-N

Hat in the Round

Project 3: Dan

The story of this hat is as easy to tell as this hat is to make! Once upon a time, a new knitter wanted a simple hat to make, so this one was designed for him. We think you will love your version of this hat as much as Dan loves his. There's nothing like a woolly hat in winter, and we can assure you that there is something extra cosy about a hat you have made yourself. You can play with colour and have a jazzy contrast brim (as in our orange and pink version... have you noticed we like orange and pink?!) or make it in one colour if that's what you fancy. We have added fun pom poms to both our versions, but you can rock a pom pom free version if you like!

Notes on Construction:

This hat is knit from the brim up to the crown. You will start on 40cm / 16" circular needles and change to either DPNs or Magic Loop when the stitches no longer easily stretch around the 40cm / 16" needle. You will use two types of decreases to make a neat decrease up to the top.

Techniques You Need to Know:
- Casting on (see page 12)
- Knit stitch (see page 14)
- Purl stitch (see page 18)
- Using stitch markers (see page 63)
- Small circumference knitting in the round (DPNs or Magic Loop) (see page 64-67)
- Knitting in the round on 40cm / 16" circular needles (see page 60)

Techniques Introduced:
- Decreasing (k2tog and ssk)
- Long-tail cast-on
- Changing colour (optional)
- Pom poms (optional)

Bonus Info:

Decreasing means reducing the number of stitches you have. In this pattern, you decrease to form the crown of the hat. It's a simple technique and is used in all sorts of places, whenever you want fewer stitches on your needle to make your knitting fit whichever part of the body you are making it for. When you come to the decreases at the top of the hat, you'll notice that we use two different types. K2tog (knit two together) is the easiest and most frequently used decrease. It's very simple to achieve and is more or less what it sounds like: you knit two stitches at the same time. K2tog creates a decrease which leans to the right. This is where ssk comes in! Ssk (slip slip knit) is a left-leaning decrease that mirrors k2tog. Use them together and you get lovely neat decreases like the ones in this hat! The number of stitches decreased or the total number of stitches left on the needle after a decrease round is identified in italics as a stitch count at the end of the round.

Top Tip! Negative Ease

If a finished item has 'negative ease' this means that it is smaller than the area it is intended to fit. This is common in hats as you often want them to be snug! If you look at the size of head the hat is intended to fit compared to the finished measurements of the hat, you'll notice there's a difference in size. The idea is that the hat should stretch a little over your head so that it stays on. If you aren't sure which size to make, perhaps measure a hat that fits you well and make the size with the closest finished measurements.

Sizes: 1 (2, 3)

To fit head circumference up to: 52 (56, 60) cm / 20½ (22, 23½)"

Finished circumference: 44 (48, 52) cm / 17½ (19, 20½)" - to be worn with 6 – 8 cm / 2½ - 3" negative ease.

Finished height (with brim folded): 20.5 (22.5, 25.5) cm / 8 (9, 10)"

Yarn: BC Garn Semilla Grosso (aran / heavy worsted weight; 100% organic wool; 80 m / 87 yds per 50 g ball)

Three Colour Version (shown in size 1)
Shades:

A: Burnt Orange (115); 1 (1, 1) ball

B: Magenta (109); 2 (2, 2) balls

C (for optional pom pom): Grey (101); 1 (1, 1) ball

Note: only 10 g of yarn is required for pom pom

Single Colour Version (shown in size 3)
Shades:

A: Grey (109); 2 (2, 2) balls

B (for optional pom pom): Burnt Orange (115); 1 (1, 1) ball

Note: only 10 g of yarn is required for pom pom

Gauge: 20 sts & 24 rounds = 10 cm / 4" over stocking stitch worked in the round on 4.5 mm needles after blocking.

Needles: 3.75 mm / US 5 **AND** 4.5 mm / US 7 circular needles, 40 cm / 16" length

4.5 mm / US 7 DPNs **OR** 80 cm / 32" length circular needle for working Magic Loop for crown shaping.

Always use a needle size that will result in the correct gauge after blocking.

Notions: 4 stitch markers (one unique for beginning of round), pom pom maker, tapestry needle

PATTERN BEGINS
BRIM

Using smaller circular needle, yarn A, and the long-tail method, cast on 88 (96, 104) sts.

Join for working in the round, being careful not to twist. PM to indicate beg of round.

Round 1: [K2, p2] to end.

Repeat round 1 (creating 2x2 ribbing) until piece measures 10 cm / 4" from cast-on edge. **Note:** This is long enough for a folded brim. If you would like an unfolded brim then you can work ribbing until brim measures 5 cm / 2".

Cut yarn A, leaving a 15 cm / 6" tail to weave in later.

Alternatively, for single colour version, continue in yarn A.

BODY

Change to larger needles and join yarn B (or continue in yarn A for single colour version). Work in St st in the round (knit every round) until piece measures 19 (20, 22) cm / 7½ (8, 8½)" (or desired length) from cast-on edge.

CROWN SHAPING

Round 1: [K1, ssk, k17 (19, 21), k2tog, PM] three times, k1, ssk, k17 (19, 21), k2tog. *80 (88, 96) sts*

Round 2: Knit.

Round 3: [K1, ssk, k to 2 sts before marker, k2tog, SM] four times. *8 sts dec*

Repeat rounds 2-3 until 16 sts remain.

Note: As you knit the crown you will eventually need to change to DPNs or long circular needle for Magic Loop when you have too few stitches to comfortably work on 40 cm / 16" needles.

Next round: [K2tog] 8 times. *8 sts*

FINISHING

Cut yarn, leaving a 20 cm / 8" tail. Thread the tail onto a tapestry needle, draw it through the remaining stitches and pull tight to close. Bring the tail to the inside of the hat and weave it in.

Weave in any remaining ends and block to measurements.

Optional pom pom:

Using yarn C (or yarn B for single colour version) make a pom pom using the tutorial instructions.

Attach pom pom to top of hat using threads from tie around the centre, using a tapestry needle. Weave in ends inside hat.

a. Finished circumference: 44 (48, 52) cm / 17½ (19, 20½)"

b. Finished height (with brim folded): 20.5 (22.5, 25.5) cm / 8 (9, 10)"

How to do a Long-Tail Cast-On

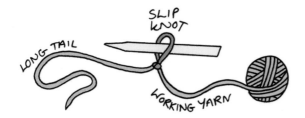

1. Make a slip knot leaving a generous tail and place on needle. Your tail will need to be at least 3 times the length of the project's finished measurement to make the required number of stitches.

2. Arrange yarn on left hand, with the long tail over thumb and the working yarn threaded behind index finger.

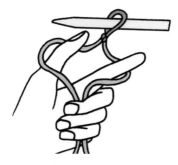

3. Bend fingers to trap the long tail and working yarn and hold secure.

4. Scoop needle from left to right to pick up tail yarn on left side of thumb.

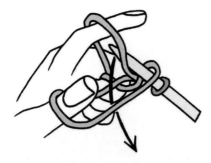

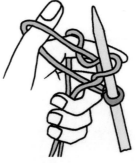

5. Lean needle to pick up working yarn looped over index finger.

6. Draw working yarn through to create stitch on needle.

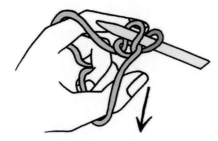

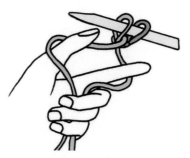

7. Make sure your new stitch is snug on the needle by gently pulling yarn tail with thumb in the direction shown. Make sure not to pull too hard, you don't want your stitches to be too tight.

8. Ensure tail yarn and working yarn are arranged as detailed in Step 2 and repeat Steps 3 -7 to cast on required number of stitches.

Joining New Yarn

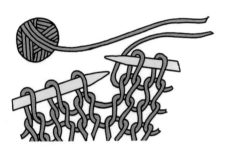

1. Leave a tail of at least 20cm / 8" of your 'old' yarn (shown in blue) and drop this yarn. Pick up the new yarn, ready to knit.

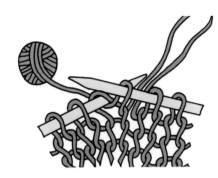

2. Insert right-hand needle into next stitch to knit as normal but wrap with new yarn. Draw needle through to make stitch.

3. Continue knitting with new yarn, pulling tail ends to tighten the stitches if necessary. Weave in loose ends at end of project.

Threading Yarn Through Remaining Stitches

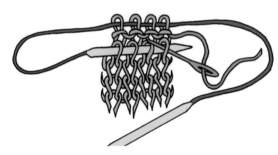

1. Cut yarn, leaving a 30cm / 12" tail and thread onto tapestry needle. Pass tapestry needle through first stitch on needle purlwise.

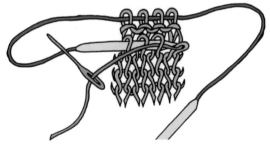

2. Continue for each stitch, inserting tapestry needle purlwise and drawing yarn through.

3. After all your stitches have been secured with the tail, gently slide your stitches off the knitting needle. Finish by pulling yarn to gather stitches together and secure by weaving in end on wrong side.

Knit Two Together (k2tog) - Right-Leaning Decrease

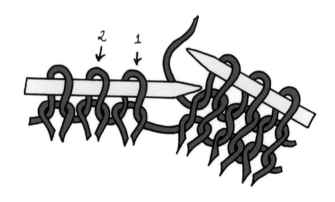

1. This method of decreasing uses all the same actions as a standard knit stitch, but the first and second stitch on your left needle are worked together.

2. Insert right-hand needle into these two stitches. First enter the second stitch from front to back, then the first in the same manner, as shown.

3. Wrap or pick yarn as you would for a knit stitch.

4. Draw the yarn through, and drop two stitches off left-hand needle.

Slip Slip Knit (ssk) - Left-Leaning Decrease

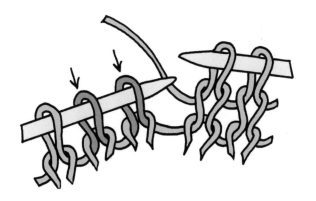

1. The arrows indicate the stitches you will work for this decrease.

2. Slip next two stitches, one after the other, from left to right needle knitwise (inserting the needle into each stitch as if to knit but passing the stitch to the right needle without knitting). See page 85 for our how-to on slipping stitches.

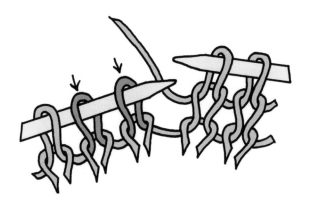

3. Now slip these stitches back onto the left needle, one at a time. They will now be twisted as shown.

4. Knit through both stitches by inserting your needle through both from front to back as shown. The stitches are twisted so you are knitting through the back loop. Knit through both of these stitches.

5. Ta da!

How to Make a Pom Pom!

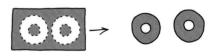

1. Cut two donut shapes from stiff card. The diameter of these determines the size of your pom poms. The hole in the centre will need to be big enough to pass yarn through easily.

2. Hold the two circles together and wrap yarn around both the circles. Tip! You can cut a slit through both circles to make this easier.

3. Wrap yarn until you cannot fit any more yarn through the hole.

4. Snip the yarn between the cardboard circles.

5. Carefully separate the two cardboard circles and knot a strand of yarn tightly around the yarn between them.

6. Give the pom pom a hair cut and snip any stray strands, but be careful not to snip the long strands from the piece of yarn you used to tie the middle of the pom pom. You can use these to attach your pom pom to your hat!

J-O-H-N
&
J-U-L-I-E-T

Cuffs in the Round

Project 4: John & Juliet

As you progress, you might discover woolly items you never knew you needed. Cuffs such as these might be one of those items! These are essentially a tube that covers your wrist and palm, plus a hole for your thumb. They leave your fingers free to knit, and you'll be surprised by the difference they can make on a chilly day. You can even layer them with mittens or gloves if you want to. They can save a too-short coat sleeve or protect skin from cold air that sneaks past short gloves and up your sleeves in winter.

Notes on Construction:

These cuffs are knit from the wrist up to the palm, leaving a gap for your thumb. They are mostly knit in the round, and for those sections you'll only be working on the right side (RS) of your work. This will make a tube of knitting. To create the thumb hole, you will work a section of the cuffs flat and then rejoin your knitting to work in the round again. This nifty trick is much easier than it sounds!

Techniques You Need to Know:
- Casting on (see page 74)
- Knit stitch (see page 14)
- Purl stitch (see page 18)
- Casting off (see page 22)
- Knitting a small circumference
  in the round (see page 64-67)
- Using stitch markers (see page 63)

Techniques Introduced:
- Slipping stitches knitwise and purlwise

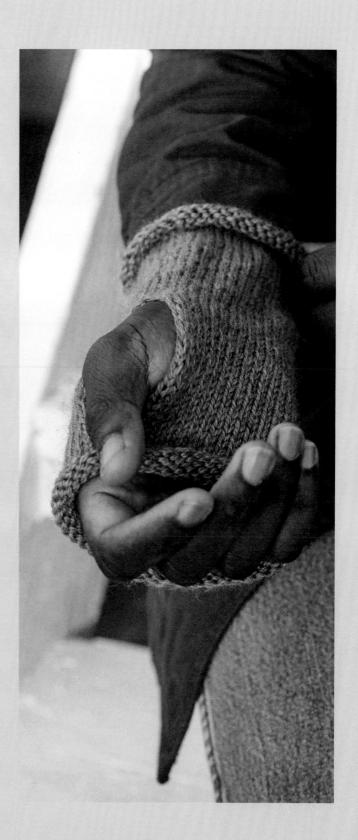

Sizes: 1 (2, 3, 4)

To fit hand circumference: 17.5 (19, 22, 24) cm / 7 (7½, 8½, 9)"

Yarn: John Arbon Textiles Viola (DK weight; 100% Merino wool; 250 m / 273 yds per 100 g skein)

Shade: Blackcurrant; 1 (1, 1, 1) skein
OR Shepherd's Warning; 1 (1, 1, 1) skein

Gauge: 22 sts & 29 rows = 10 cm / 4" over stocking stitch worked in the round on 4.5 mm needles after blocking.

Needles: 4.5 mm / US 7 DPNs **OR** 80 cm / 32" length circular needle for working Magic Loop
Always use a needle size that will result in the correct gauge after blocking.

Notions: Stitch marker, tapestry needle

PATTERN BEGINS
(make 2 alike)
HAND
Using the long-tail method, cast on 38 (42, 46, 50) sts.
Join for working in the round, being careful not to twist.
PM to indicate beg of round.

Work St st in the round (knit every round), until Hand measures 5 cm / 2" from cast-on edge.

THUMBHOLE
You will now change from working in the round to working back and forth in rows to create a thumbhole. Work the stitches as they are – no need for you to rearrange them across the needles but you will need to remove the stitch marker for now.

Row 1 (WS): Turn your work so the purl side is facing you, sl1 pwise with yarn held in front (ie. closest to you), p to end.

Row 2 (RS): Turn work so the knit side is facing you, sl1 kwise with yarn in back (ie. at the back of your work), k to end.

Rep rows 1 and 2 a further 5 (5, 6, 6) times, or until the flat Thumbhole section measures 4 (4, 5, 5) cm / 1½ (1½, 2, 2)", ending with row 2.

WRIST
You will return to working in the round again, with the knit side of the fabric facing you as follows:

Next Round (RS): Join to work in the round once again, replacing the stitch marker for the beginning of the round and k to end.

Continue to knit every round until mitt measures 23 cm / 9" (or desired length) from cast-on edge.

Cast off.

FINISHING
Weave in all loose ends and block to measurements.

a. Finished circumference: 17 (19, 21, 22.5) cm / 6¾ (7½, 8¼, 9)"

b. Finished length: 23 cm / 9"

Knit How

Slip sts kwise (with Yarn in Back)

1. Insert your right needle into the stitch you want to slip as if to knit as shown.

2. Pass stitch from left to right needle so that it's now sitting on the right needle as shown, but you haven't worked it by pulling the working yarn through. You will notice that the stitch is now sitting over the needle differently - it is 'twisted' which means the left leg of the stitch is in front and the right leg is behind. In this scenario the 'twist' is intended but sometimes you may end up with 'twisted' stitches by mistake, in which case see page 145 for our how-to fix.

3. The working yarn will pass behind the slipped stitch before continuing to work with the subsequent stitches.

Slip sts pwise (with Yarn in Back)

1. Insert your right needle into the stitch you want to slip as if to purl as shown.

2. Pass stitch from left to right so that it's now sitting on the right needle as shown, but you haven't worked it by pulling the working yarn through.

3. You can now continue working the next stitches as instructed. The working yarn will pass behind the slipped stitch before continuing to work with the subsequent stitches.

Pattern 5.1: Fiona
- Simple Cabled Scarf

Pattern 5.2: Alice
- Adventurous Cabled Scarf

F-I-O-N-A
–
A-L-I-C-E

Cabled Scarves

Many knitters get nervous about cables at first. They are pretty impressive looking, and do appear to have been created with a special sprinkling of magic. In fact they are fairly straightforward, and although they can appear complicated, they are exactly what they look like: sets of stitches swapping places to create a braid-like effect. To aid us in crossing stitches over each other, we use a cable needle. This is a short needle, often with a dip in the middle, which holds stitches either in front or behind your work while they wait to be knitted. This scarf is the perfect way to get to grips with cables and we think it's a pretty versatile one too. Embellish with pom poms, as shown in the honey version here, or leave them off for a sleeker look.

Notes on Construction:

This scarf is knit flat from short end to short end. We have two versions for you: a simpler version (shown in honey and worn by Roshni); and a more adventurous version (shown in blue and worn by Issa). You can decide which feels right for you. Or make one and then the other... there is no such thing as too many beautiful scarves!

Techniques You Need to Know:
- Casting on (see page 74)
- Knit stitch (see page 14)
- Purl stitch (see page 18)
- Casting off (see page 22)
- Slipped stitches (see page 85)
- Pom poms (optional! See page 78)

Techniques Introduced:
- Cables
- Reading from charts

Bonus Info:

Cables normally lean to the left or to the right, and are identified as either L or R alongside the number of stitches used. When you create a left-leaning cable, you hold stitches in front of your work, and when the cable has to lean right you hold stitches behind.

Top Tip! Written Instructions Vs Charts

Not all patterns are written out in the way you have encountered so far. If a pattern can be divided into sections of repeating rows, each part will often be presented in a chart of stitches.

A chart is a visual representation of the stitches, presented as a sort of table. Each stitch used is given a symbol and you work a stitch when you see its symbol in the chart. The symbols become second nature very quickly. Charts can be much easier to work from than written instructions once you get used to them, especially with cables. When you use a chart, you can get a rough idea of what your knitting should look like as you work through it. This means you can tell more easily if your stitches aren't lining up in the way they should.

If you want to use the chart for this pattern, go ahead! If it doesn't feel natural yet, stick with the written instructions. There's no right or wrong here, just whatever is most comfortable and productive for you! You will find charts again in project 8.

Pattern 5.1: Fiona
- Simple Cabled Scarf

One size: 21 cm / 8¼" wide x 190 cm / 75" long
Yarn: Quince & Co. Osprey (aran / heavy worsted weight; 100% American wool; 155 m / 170 yds per 100 g skein)
Shade: 123 Honey; 3 skeins
Gauge: 13 sts & 18 rows = 10 cm / 4" over garter stitch on 8 mm needles after blocking.
Needles: 8 mm / US 11 knitting needles
Always use a needle size that will result in the correct gauge after blocking.
Notions: Large cable needle, tapestry needle, pom pom maker

Stitch Glossary (special abbreviations you will need for this pattern):
CABLES
3/3 RC: Slip 3 sts to cable needle and hold at back of work, k3, then k3 from cable needle.
3/3 LC: Slip 3 sts to cable needle and hold at front of work, k3, then k3 from cable needle.

PATTERN BEGINS
Using the long-tail method, cast on 35 sts.
Knit 6 rows in garter stitch.

CABLE PATTERN
Starting with a RS row 1, commence cable pattern reading from the Chart (overleaf) or following Written Instructions.

Note: Slip stitches should be slipped purlwise with yarn held at back of work (pwise wyib).
WRITTEN INSTRUCTIONS FOR CHART
Row 1 (RS): K5, p2, k6, p2, k2, sl1, k2, p2, k6, p2, k5.
Row 2 (WS & all following WS rows): K7, p6, k4, p1, k4, p6, k7.
Row 3: As row 1.
Row 5: As row 1.
Row 7 (RS): K5, p2, 3/3 RC, p2, k2, sl1, k2, p2, 3/3 LC, p2, k5.
Row 8 (WS): As row 2.
Repeat rows 1-8 until scarf measures approx 186 cm / 73" from cast-on edge (completing 40 full repeats of rows 1-8 in total), ending after row 8.
Work rows 1-4 **only** once more.

Knit 6 rows in garter stitch.
Cast off all sts.

FINISHING
Weave in all loose ends and block to measurements.
Divide the remaining yarn into four equal parts, make four pom poms and securely stitch one at each corner.

a. Width: 21 cm / 8¼"
b. Length: 190 cm / 75"

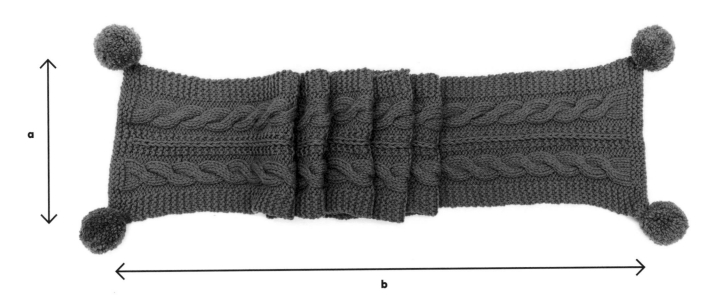

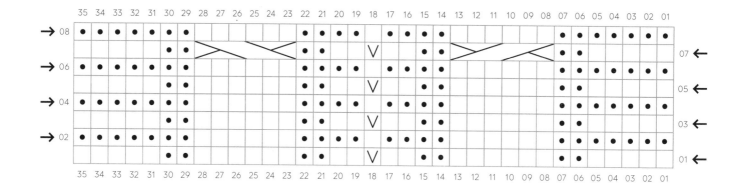

Key

	RS: knit / WS: purl
●	RS: purl / WS: knit
V	RS: slip purlwise with yarn in back
	3/3 LC
	3/3 RC

The section between these dotted lines on this image shows one full repeat of the chart.

Top Tip! Reading from Charts

Charts are written so that the symbols mirror how the knitting looks from the right side. Charts come with a key which shows the stitch that each symbol relates to. As the symbols only show the stitches from the right side, the key also explains which stitch the symbol relates to when worked from the wrong side e.g. knit on RS rows, purl on WS rows. When reading charts, for right side rows you read the symbols from right to left, in the same way that you knit a row from right to left. However for wrong side rows, you read the symbols from left to right, as indicated by the arrows.

When working charts in the round, all rows are read from right to left, as all the rows you work are right side rows.

Pattern 5.2: Alice
- Adventurous Cabled Scarf

One size: 19 cm / 7½" wide x 130 cm / 51" long
Yarn: Quince & Co. Osprey (aran / heavy worsted weight; 100% American wool; 155 m / 170 yds per 100 g skein)
Shade: Aleutian; 3 skeins
Gauge: 19 sts & 26 rows = 10 cm / 4" over Cable Pattern on 8 mm needles after blocking.
Needles: 8 mm / US 11 knitting needles
Always use a needle size that will result in the correct gauge after blocking.
Notions: Large cable needle, tapestry needle

Stitch Glossary (special abbreviations you will need for this pattern):
CABLES
3/3 RC: Slip 3 sts to cable needle and hold at back of work, k3, then k3 from cable needle.
3/3 LC: Slip 3 sts to cable needle and hold at front of work, k3, then k3 from cable needle.

PATTERN BEGINS
Using the long-tail method, cast on 35 sts.
Row 1: [K1, p1] to last st, k1.
Row 1 sets Moss Stitch.
Work a further 7 rows in Moss Stitch.

CABLE PATTERN
Starting with a RS row 1, commence cable pattern reading from the Chart (overleaf) or following Written Instructions below.
Note: Slip stitches should be slipped purlwise with yarn held at back of work (pwise wyib).
WRITTEN INSTRUCTIONS FOR CHART
Row 1 (RS): K1, [p1, sl1] twice, p2, k6, p2, [sl1, p1] 3 times, p1, k6, p2, [sl1, p1] twice, k1.
Row 2 (WS): [P1, k1] twice, p1, k2, p6, k2, [p1, k1] twice, p1, k2, p6, k2, [p1, k1] twice, p1.
Rows 3-6: Rep rows 1-2.
Row 7: K1, [p1, sl1] twice, p2, 3/3 RC, p2, [sl1, p1] twice, p1, p2, 3/3 LC, p2, [sl1, p1] twice, k1.
Row 8 (WS): As row 2.
Rep rows 1-8, working a total of 39 reps of rows 1-8, then work Rows 1-4 **only** once more.

Work 8 rows in Moss Stitch.
Cast off in Moss Stitch pattern.

FINISHING
Weave in all loose ends and block to measurements.

a. Width: 19 cm / 7½"
b. Length: 130 cm / 51"

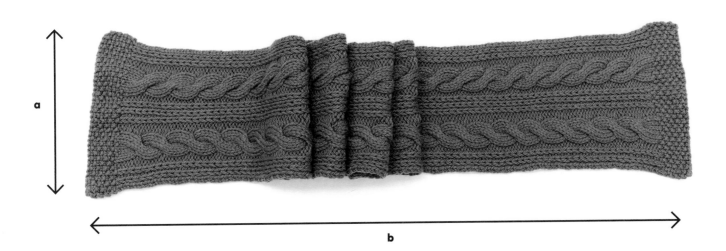

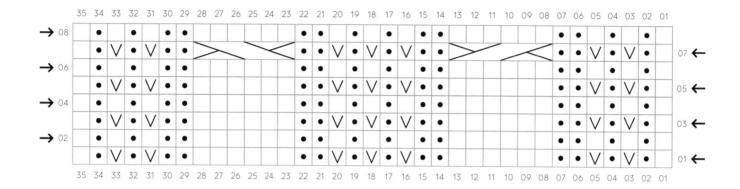

Key

	RS: knit / WS: purl
●	RS: purl / WS: knit
V	RS: slip purlwise with yarn in back
⟩⟨	3/3 LC
⟩⟨	3/3 RC

The section between these dotted lines on this image shows one full repeat of the chart.

Left-Leaning Cable (Stitches Held in Front)

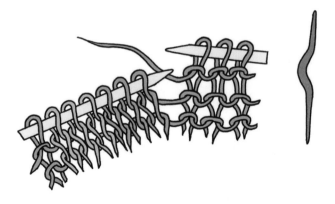

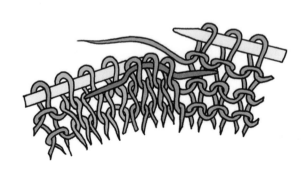

1. Stitches shown in fuschia will pass in front. Stitches shown in pale pink will pass behind.

2. Slide first three stitches, one at a time, off left-hand needle onto cable needle. Arrange cable needle to sit at front of work and leave it there for now.

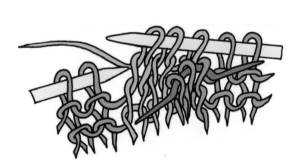

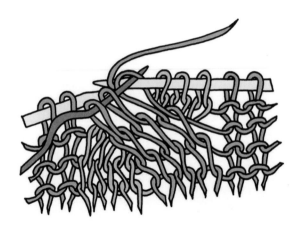

3. Knit next three stitches on left-hand needle.

4. Using cable needle as if it were your left-hand needle, knit the three stitches held on cable needle onto right-hand needle.

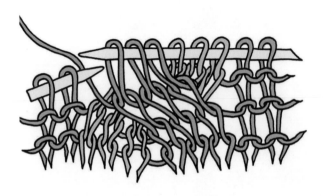

5. Your cable is complete.

Right-Leaning Cable (Stitches Held Behind)

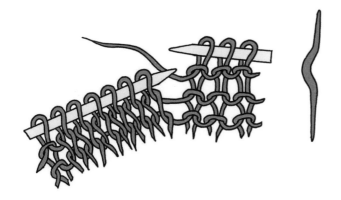

1. Stitches shown in teal will pass behind. Stitches shown in olive will pass in front.

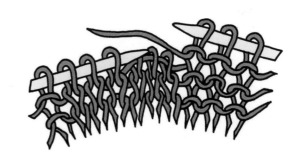

2. Slide first three stitches, one at a time, off left-hand needle onto cable needle. Arrange cable needle to sit at back of work and leave it there for now.

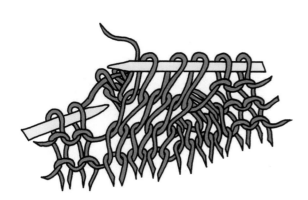

3. Knit next three stitches on left-hand needle.

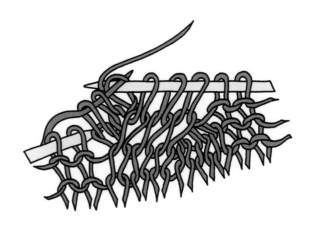

4. Using cable needle as if it were your left-hand needle, knit the three stitches held on cable needle onto right-hand needle.

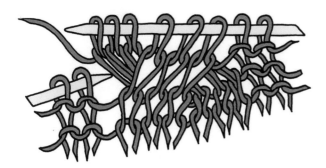

5. Your cable is complete.

Project 6

R-O-S-A

First Mittens in the Round

Fancy treating yourself to snuggly hands? These mittens are great fun, unisex, and the contrast colour is an excellent way to use up leftover yarn. You'll praise these cute mitts on icy days when fingerless gloves aren't enough. The trickiest part of this project is the thumb, but not only will you make these thumbs, you'll be giving everyone the thumbs up to show them off. To make the thumb you will be increasing (adding stitches) and then setting those stitches aside while you finish the hand. The fun thing about doing the thumb last is that, although it may be fiddly, it's very quick once you get going because there are so few stitches.

Notes on Construction:
Knit in the round using either Magic Loop or DPNs, whichever you find easier. These mittens start at the cuff and finish at the fingertips. The thumb is completed last.

Techniques You Need to Know:
- Casting on (see page 74)
- Knit stitch (see page 14)
- Purl stitch (see page 18)
- Knitting in the round
  (DPNs or Magic Loop, see page 64-67)
- K2tog (see page 76)
- Reading garter ridges (see page 26)

Techniques Introduced:
- Increasing (M1L and M1R)
- Garter stitch in the round
- Picking up stitches

Bonus Info:
Making garter stitch in the round can be a little confusing at first. Garter knit flat requires only one type of stitch; either all purl rows or all knit rows. In the round, however, you need to work alternating knit and purl rounds to create the same effect. If you think about the fact that you always work on the right side (RS) of the fabric when you knit in the round this might start to make more sense!

Top Tip! Increasing

Increasing means adding extra stitches. In this case you increase to create space for your thumb. The increased thumb stitches are known as a gusset. As with decreases, there are several types of increases. This pattern uses two types: a left-leaning one called Make 1 Left (abbreviated to M1L), and a right-leaning one called Make 1 Right (M1R). As with decreasing the total number of stitches you should have on your needle after an increase round is identified in italics as a stitch count at the end of the instructions for that round.

Pattern 6: Rosa

Sizes: 1 (2, 3)
To fit hand circumference: 18 (20, 23) cm / 7 (8, 9)"
- worn with 1-2 cm / ⅓-¾" negative ease
Finished circumference: 17 (18, 22) cm / 6¾ (7, 8½)"
Length: Adjust to fit
Yarn: Retrosaria Rosa Pomar Beiroa (DK weight;
100% Portuguese wool; 250 m / 273 yds per 100g skein)
Shades:
A: 478 (rust); 1 (1, 1) skein
B: 734 (lilac); 1 (1, 1) skein
Gauge: 20 sts & 26 rows = 10 cm / 4" over stocking stitch
worked in the round on 4 mm needles after blocking.
Needles: 3.75 mm / US 4 DPNs **OR** circular needle, minimum
80 cm / 32" length for working Magic Loop
4 mm / US 6 DPNs **OR** circular needle, minimum 80 cm /
32" length for working Magic Loop
Always use a needle size that will result in the correct
gauge after blocking.
Notions: 4 stitch markers (one unique for beginning of
round), waste yarn, tapestry needle

Notes: Where only one number is given this applies to all sizes.

PATTERN BEGINS
CUFF
Using smaller needles, yarn A, and the long-tail method,
cast on 32 (36, 44) sts. Join for working in the round, being
careful not to twist. PM to indicate beg of round.
Round 1: Purl.
Round 2: Knit.
Rep rounds 1 and 2 a further 10 times (11 garter ridges in total).
Break yarn B leaving a 15 cm / 6" tail to weave in later.

HAND
Change to larger needles and continue in yarn B only as follows:
Work 5 rounds in St st (knit every round).

Commence Thumb Gusset:
Note: The set up for the thumb gusset is different for the
right and left hands – ensure you work one of each – it's
very easy to forget!

Left Hand ONLY
Set-up round: K to last 2 sts of round, PM, M1L, PM, k2. *1 st inc*

Right Hand ONLY
Set-up round: K2, PM, M1L, PM, k to end of round. *1 st inc*

BOTH Hands Again
Round 1: Knit all sts, slipping the markers as you come to them.
Round 2: K to marker, SM, M1R, k1, M1L, SM, k to end. *2 sts inc*
Rounds 3-4: Knit, slipping markers as you come to them.
Round 5: K to marker, SM, M1R, k to marker, M1L, SM, k to end. *2 sts inc*
Rep rounds 3-5 a further 3 (4, 5) times until there are 11 (13, 15) sts between the markers. *43 (49, 59) sts in total on the needles; 11 (13, 15) gusset sts*
Knit 1 round, slipping markers as you come to them.

Left Hand ONLY
Next round: K to marker, remove marker, place next 11 (13, 15) sts (thumb stitches) onto waste yarn (see page 115), remove marker, k to end. *32 (36, 44) sts*

Right Hand ONLY
Next round: K2, remove marker, place next 11 (13, 15) sts (thumb stitches) onto waste yarn (see page 115), remove marker, k to end. *32 (36, 44) sts*

BOTH Hands Again
Work in St st until piece measures 15.5 (18, 20) cm / 6¼ (7, 7¾)" from cast-on edge, or 4 cm / 1½" less than desired length.

Shape Mitten Top
Set-up round: [K8 (9, 11), PM] 3 times, k to end. 4 markers placed – beginning of round marker plus 3 new markers.
Note: Use the contrast marker to indicate beg of round.
Dec round: [K to 2 sts before marker, k2tog] 4 times. *4 sts dec*
Next round: Knit.
Rep last 2 rounds until 16 sts remain.
Rep Dec round **only** until 8 sts remain.
Cut yarn, leaving a 15 cm / 6" tail. Thread the tail onto a tapestry needle, draw it through the remaining sts and pull tight to close, taking the tail through to the inside.

THUMB
Set-up round: Place 11 (13, 15) held thumb gusset sts on larger needle. Rejoin yarn B leaving a 15 cm / 6" tail and k across these sts, pick up and k3 sts in gap. Join for working in the round and PM to indicate beg of round. *14 (16, 18) sts*
Work 13 (16, 19) rounds in St st or until Thumb measures 2 cm / ¾" less than desired length.

Thumb Decreases:
Round 1: [K2, k2tog] 3 (4, 4) times, k2 (0, 2). *11 (12, 14) sts*
Round 2: [K1, k2tog] 3 (4, 4) times, k2 (0, 2). *8 (8, 10) sts*
Round 3: [K1, k2tog] 2 (2, 3) times, k2 (2, 1). *6 (6, 7) sts*
Cut yarn, leaving a 15 cm / 6" tail. Thread the tail onto a tapestry needle, draw it through the remaining stitches and pull tight to close, taking the tail through to the inside.

FINISHING
Weave in any remaining ends and use the long tail at the Thumb to close any gaps. Block to measurements.

a. Finished Circumference: 17 (18, 22) cm / 6¾ (7, 8½)"

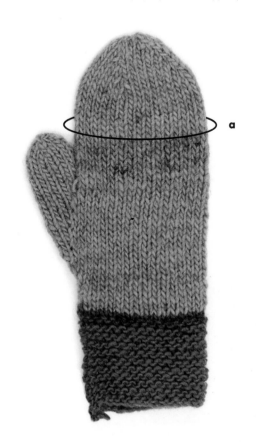

Make 1 Left (M1L)

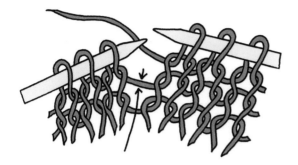

1. Identify the strand between two adjacent stitches.

2. Using right-hand needle pick up strand from front to back. This strand becomes the new stitch.

3. Place this stitch on your left-hand needle as shown. The left leg of the stitch should sit behind the needle, and the right leg should sit in front as with your other stitches.

4. Knit through back loop as shown. To do this, insert your needle from behind so that the legs of the stitches cross over.

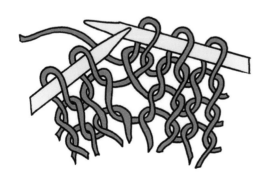

5. One stitch increased.

Make 1 Right (M1R)

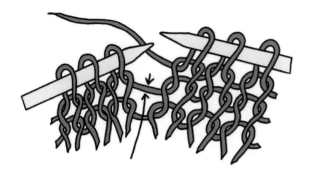

1. Identify the strand between two adjacent stitches.

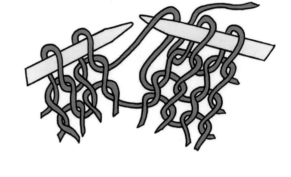

2. Using right-hand needle, pick up strand from front to back. This strand will become the new stitch.

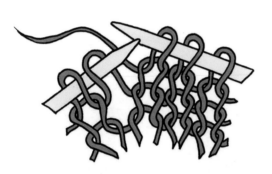

3. Place stitch on left-hand needle as pictured.

4. Knit stitch.

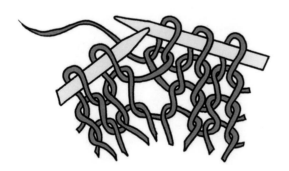

5. One stitch increased

Picking Up Thumb Stitches

1. Split your stitches evenly over your needles. You will be following the arrow and picking up stitches where indicated. Insert your left-hand needle into the centre of the next stitch from front to back.

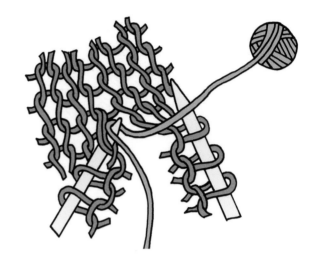

2. Wrap your working yarn around the needle.

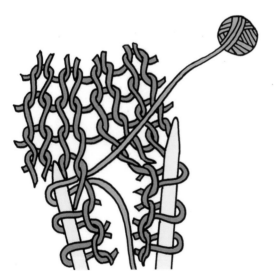

3. Pull the yarn back through the centre of the stitch. You have now picked up one stitch.

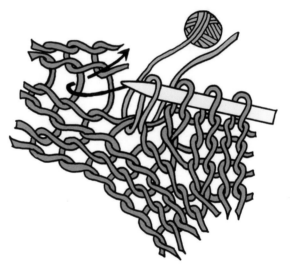

4. Repeat steps 1-3 until you have picked up the correct number of stitches.

Pattern 7.1: Chris
- First Jumper

Pattern 7.2: James
- Waffle Jumper

C-H-R-I-S
–
J-A-M-E-S

Jumpers

Sometimes we like our jumpers (or sweaters!) boxy and a little roomy, and sometimes not so much. This jumper can be either depending on the size you choose to make, and suits most shapes.. There is something very satisfying about a simple jumper, you can throw it on with almost anything and we can guarantee that this one is a real compliment-grabber. There are two versions for you to choose from. One is stockinette stitch and ribbing, with some punchy colour blocking (shown in rust and pink on Ayesha). You can make this version in one colour if you want to... or add more colours if that's how you roll. If you are feeling slightly more adventurous, then you can try the version featuring a nice easy bit of waffle texture over the yoke (the part of the jumper that covers the upper chest and shoulders) as shown in yellow on Issa. And, as always, we encourage you to experiment if that's something that appeals. Why not just have your cuffs and neckband in a contrast colour? Or you could make your sleeves a different colour to the body, and your cuffs another shade entirely. Endless possibilities.

Top Tip! Picking Up Stitches

Picking up stitches is another very handy technique that is used in a myriad of ways. It also creates a satisfyingly neat join with no need for seams! For this jumper, you will pick up stitches for your sleeves and again to finish off your neckband. These are larger numbers of stitches to pick up in one go than for your mitten thumbs, so we recommend placing locking stitch markers at even intervals along the area you are picking up. This helps you to divide and space your picked-up stitches evenly. For example, if you have to pick up 40 stitches, you could place 3 markers to split the area into 4 equal sections to make sure you pick up 10 stitches per section and you're all done!

Notes on Construction:

This jumper is worked from the bottom up, meaning you start with the ribbing at the bottom of the body then work upwards toward the shoulders. You will work this entire lower section in the round, and then change to working back and forth in rows over the two halves of the stitches for the front and back. These will then be joined at the top of the shoulders, leaving an opening for the arms and neck. Next, you will pick up stitches for the sleeves, which are then worked downwards in the round. Once these are complete, you will pick up stitches for the neckline ribbing, and voila! Your first ever jumper.

Bonus Info: Positive and Negative Ease

This jumper is intended to be boxy and loose-fitting. This means the final measurements incorporate a lot of 'positive ease', meaning extra space. If you compare the difference between the chest size that each jumper size is intended to fit with the garment's finished measurements, you'll see there's a difference between them. If you would like a more fitted look (as shown in the waffle version on Issa), you can make a smaller size. Maybe measure a favourite comfy jumper and make the size which has the closest finished measurements. Don't forget your gauge swatch!

Techniques You Need to Know:
  - Casting on (see page 74)
  - Knit stitch (see page 14)
  - Purl stitch (see page 18)
  - Knitting in the round (see page 60)
  - Knitting small circumferences in the round (DPNs or Magic Loop, see page 64-67)
  - Ssk and k2tog decreases (see page 76)
  - M1L and M1R increases (see page 103 & 104)
  - 2x2 ribbing (see page 72)
  - Picking up stitches (see page 105)

Techniques Introduced:
  - Putting stitches on hold
  - Three-needle cast-off

Sizes: 1 (2, 3, 4, 5, 6, 7, 8, 9)
Finished bust circumference: 96.5 (105.5, 114.5, 125.5, 136.5, 145.5, 155, 165, 178) cm / 38 (41½, 45, 49½, 54, 57½, 61, 65, 70)" - to be worn with up to 25 cm / 10" positive ease.
Ayesha has 86 cm / 34" bust, stands 166 cm / 5'5" tall and is wearing a size 2.
Issa has 86 cm / 34" chest, stands 187 cm / 6'1" tall and is wearing a size 3.
Yarn: De Rerum Natura Gilliatt (worsted weight; 100% Merino wool; 250 m / 273 yds per 100 g ball)
Chris (Colour Block version, shown on Ayesha)
Shades:
A: Fauve (rust); 3 (3, 4, 4, 4, 5, 5, 5, 6) balls
B: Argile (pink); 1 (1, 2, 2, 2, 2, 2, 3, 3) balls
James (Waffle Stitch version, shown on Issa)
Shade: Golden (yellow); 4 (4, 4, 5, 5, 6, 6, 7, 7) balls
Gauge: 18 sts & 24 rows = 10cm / 4" over stocking stitch worked in the round on 4.5 mm needles after blocking.
Needles: 4mm / US 6 **and** 4.5 mm / US 7 circular needle, 80 cm / 32" length
4mm / US 6 **and** 4.5 mm / US 7 DPNs **OR** minimum 100 cm / 40" circular needle for Magic Loop, for working the Sleeves, Neckband and 3-needle cast off. If preferred the Neckband may be worked with a 40 cm / 16" length circular needle instead.
Always use a needle size that will result in the correct gauge after blocking.
Notions: 2 stitch markers in different colours, waste yarn or stitch holder, tapestry needle
Notes: Two versions of this jumper are given - Chris, shown in two colours, with a contrast colour yoke, and James, in a single shade with a textured yoke. The body of the sweater is worked identically for both versions to the yoke - take care to follow the correct yoke instructions for your preferred version when indicated. Sleeves are worked identically for both versions.

Stitch Glossary
2x2 Rib in the round
Round 1: [K2, p2] to end.
Rep round 1 for pattern.

PATTERN BEGINS
LOWER RIB BAND
Using the larger 80 cm / 32" circular needle, yarn A if working Colour Block Version, and the long-tail method, cast on 172 (188, 204, 224, 244, 260, 276, 292, 316) sts. Join for working in the round, being careful not to twist. PM to indicate beg of round.
Next Round: [K2, p2] to end.
Work 2x2 Rib as set for 5 cm / 2".
Next Round: Purl.

MAIN BODY
Work St st in the round (knit every round), until piece measures 30.5 (30.5, 33, 33, 33, 35.5, 38, 40.5, 40.5) cm / 12 (12, 13, 13, 13, 14, 15, 16, 16)" from cast-on edge, or until body measures 2.5 cm / 1" less than desired finished length from underarm. If you want a longer jumper you can work extra here, and if you want a cropped jumper then work less!

Now you need to follow instructions based on whether you would like to work the waffle stitch yoke (as in the yellow sample) or the colour block yoke (seen in the rust and pink version). You can of course work the waffle stitch in a different colour if you are feeling adventurous, or just make a plain jumper all in one colour without the stitch pattern. You are the master of your jumper destiny!

COLOUR BLOCK VERSION ONLY

Cut yarn A leaving a 15 cm / 6" tail and join yarn B leaving a 15 cm / 6" tail.

Continue to work St st in the round (knit every round) using your new shade until yarn B section measures 2.5 cm / 1".

Divide for Front and Back

Divide the sts and prepare for working back and forth in rows as follows:

Split row (RS): K86 (94, 102, 112, 122, 130, 138, 146, 158) sts (half of your total sts), then place remaining 86 (94, 102, 112, 122, 130, 138, 146, 158) sts on waste yarn or a stitch holder to be worked later. Turn work so WS is facing (so you can see purl bumps) and continue working in rows across 86 (94, 102, 112, 122, 130, 138, 146, 158) Front sts only.

Next row (WS): Purl.

FRONT

Work St st flat in rows as follows:

Row 1 (RS): Knit.

Row 2 (WS): Purl.

Rep rows 1-2 until yarn B section measures 11.5 (11.5, 11.5, 12.5, 12.5, 12.5, 14, 14, 14) cm / 4½ (4½, 4½, 5, 5, 5, 5½, 5½, 5½)" ending with a WS row.

Divide for Front Neck Shaping

Next row (RS): Work St st flat as set over 36 (40, 44, 48, 53, 56, 60, 64, 69) sts and place these sts on a length of waste yarn or stitch holder, cast off next 14 (14, 14, 16, 16, 18, 18, 18, 20) sts, k36 (40, 44, 48, 53, 56, 60, 64, 69) sts to end of row. Turn so WS is facing and continue on remaining 36 (40, 44, 48, 53, 56, 60, 64, 69) sts for Right Front.

Next row (WS): Purl.

Right Front Neck

Continue in St st as set (knitting RS rows, purling WS rows), and **AT THE SAME TIME** shape the Right Front neckline as follows:

Row 1 (RS): Cast off 2 (2, 2, 2, 2, 3, 3, 3) sts, k to end.

Row 2 (WS): Purl.

Rep last 2 rows a further 1 (2, 2, 2, 3, 3, 2, 2, 2) times. *32 (34, 38, 42, 45, 48, 51, 55, 60) sts*

Next row (RS)(Dec): K1, ssk, k to end. *1 st dec*

Next row (WS): Purl.

Rep last 2 rows a further 1 (1, 2, 3, 2, 2, 2, 2, 4) times. *30 (32, 35, 38, 42, 45, 48, 52, 55) sts*

Continue in St st (knitting RS rows and purling WS rows) as

set until yarn B section measures 19 (20, 21, 21.5, 24, 24, 25.5, 28, 29) cm / 7½ (8, 8¼, 8½, 9½, 9½, 10, 11, 11½)" ending with a RS row.

Place rem 30 (32, 35, 38, 42, 45, 48, 52, 55) sts on waste yarn or stitch holder.

Left Front Neck

With WS facing, place the 36 (40, 44, 48, 53, 56, 60, 64, 69) held Front sts on the 80 cm / 32" circular needle. Rejoin yarn at neck edge, continue working in yarn B as set, and **AT THE SAME TIME** shape the Left Front neckline as follows:

Row 1 (WS): Cast off 2 (2, 2, 2, 2, 2, 3, 3, 3) sts purlwise, p to end.

Row 2 (RS): Knit.

Rep last 2 rows a further 0 (1, 1, 1, 2, 2, 1, 1, 1) times, then work Row 1 **only** once more. *32 (34, 38, 42, 45, 48, 51, 55, 60) sts*

Next row (RS)(Dec): K to last 3 sts, k2tog, k1. *1 st dec*

Next row (WS): Purl.

Rep last 2 rows a further 1 (1, 2, 3, 2, 2, 2, 2, 4) times. *30 (32, 35, 38, 42, 45, 48, 52, 55) sts*

Continue straight in St st as set until yarn B section measures 19 (20, 21, 21.5, 24, 24, 25.5, 28, 29) cm / 7½ (8, 8¼, 8½, 9½, 9½, 10, 11, 11½)", ending with a RS row.

Place rem 30 (32, 35, 38, 42, 45, 48, 52, 55) sts on waste yarn or stitch holder.

BACK

With RS facing, place the 86 (94, 102, 112, 122, 130, 138, 146, 158) held Back sts on the larger 80 cm / 32" circular needle. Rejoin yarn B and work back and forth in rows of St st until yarn B section measures 19 (20, 21, 21.5, 24, 24, 25.5, 28, 29) cm / 7½ (8, 8¼, 8½, 9½, 9½, 10, 11, 11½)" to match Front in length, ending with a WS row.

Next Row (RS): K30 (32, 35, 38, 42, 45, 48, 52, 55) sts then place them on hold for right shoulder, cast off next 26 (30, 32, 36, 38, 40, 42, 42, 48) Back sts (these will be the back of your neck), k30 (32, 35, 38, 42, 45, 48, 52, 55) remaining left shoulder sts to end and place sts on hold.

JOIN SHOULDERS

Work a 3-needle cast off to join the shoulder as follows: Place held front and back Right shoulder sts onto two different larger DPNs or circular needles. With RS together (so wrong sides are visible to you), join yarn at neck edge and work 3-needle cast off over front and back right shoulder sts. Repeat for Left shoulder sts.

WAFFLE VERSION ONLY
Set-up round: K86 (94, 102, 112, 122, 130, 138, 146, 158), M1L, PM (using a marker in a different colour to the beg of round marker so you can tell them apart), k to end, M1L. *174 (190, 206, 226, 246, 262, 278, 294, 318) sts; 87 (95, 103, 113, 123, 131, 139, 147, 159) each for Front and Back.*

Work Waffle Stitch in the round as follows:
Round 1: *K2, p1, [k1, p1] to 2 sts before next marker, k2; rep from * once more.
Round 2: Knit.
Rounds 1-2 set Waffle Stitch in the round.
Continue working reps of rounds 1 - 2 until Waffle Stitch section measures 2.5 cm / 1" ending with round 2.

Divide for Front and Back
Divide the sts and prepare for working back and forth in rows as follows:
Split row (RS): Work Waffle Stitch pattern as set to marker. Remove marker, place next 87 (95, 103, 113, 123, 131, 139, 147, 159) sts on waste yarn or a stitch holder to be worked later, remove beg of round marker. Turn your work so WS is facing and continue in rows across the 87 (95, 103, 113, 123, 131, 139, 147, 159) Front sts only.

Next row (WS): Purl.

FRONT
Work Waffle Stitch flat in rows as follows:
Row 1 (RS): K2, p1, [k1, p1] to last 2 sts, k2.
Row 2 (WS): Purl.
Rep rows 1-2 until Waffle Stitch section measures 11.5 (11.5, 11.5, 12.5, 12.5, 12.5, 14, 14, 14) cm / 4½ (4½, 4½, 5, 5, 5, 5½, 5½, 5½)", ending with a WS row.

Divide for Front Neck Shaping
Next row (RS): Work Waffle Stitch as set over next 36 (40, 44, 48, 53, 56, 60, 64, 69) sts and place these sts on a length of waste yarn or stitch holder, cast off next 15 (15, 15, 17, 17, 19, 19, 19, 21) sts, k36 (40, 44, 48, 53, 56, 60, 64, 69) sts to end of row. Turn so WS is facing and continue on remaining 36 (40, 44, 48, 53, 56, 60, 64, 69) sts for Right Front.
Next row (WS): Purl.

Right Front Neck
Continue in Waffle Stitch as set, and **AT THE SAME TIME** shape the Right Front neckline as follows:
Row 1 (RS): Cast off 2 (2, 2, 2, 2, 2, 3, 3, 3) sts, continue in pattern to end.
Row 2 (WS): Purl.
Repeat rows 1-2 a further 1 (2, 2, 2, 3, 3, 2, 2, 2) times. *32 (34, 38, 42, 45, 48, 51, 55, 60) sts*

Next row (RS)(Dec): K1, ssk, continue in pattern to end. *1 st dec*
Next row (WS): Purl.
Repeat last 2 rows a further 1 (1, 2, 3, 2, 2, 2, 2, 4) times. *30 (32, 35, 38, 42, 45, 48, 52, 55) sts*
Next row (WS): Purl.

Continue straight in Waffle Stitch as set until Waffle Stitch section measures 19 (20, 21, 21.5, 24, 24, 25.5, 28, 29) cm / 7½ (8, 8¼, 8½, 9½, 9½, 10, 11, 11½)", ending with a RS row.
Place rem 30 (32, 35, 38, 42, 45, 48, 52, 55) sts on waste yarn or stitch holder.

Left Front Neck
With WS facing, place the k36 (40, 44, 48, 53, 56, 60, 64, 69) held Front sts on larger 80 cm / 32" circular needle. Rejoin yarn at neck edge, continue working Waffle Stitch as set, and **AT THE SAME TIME** shape the Left Front neckline as follows:

Row 1 (WS): Cast off 2 (2, 2, 2, 2, 3, 3, 3) sts, p to end.
Row 2 (RS): Work in pattern to end.
Rep last 2 rows a further 0 (1, 1, 1, 2, 2, 1, 1, 1) times, then work Row 1 only once more. *32 (34, 38, 42, 45, 48, 51, 55, 60) sts*

Next row (RS)(Dec): Patt to last 3 sts, k2tog, k1. *1 st dec*
Next row (WS): Purl.
Repeat last 2 rows a further 1 (1, 2, 3, 2, 2, 2, 4) times. *30 (32, 35, 38, 42, 45, 48, 52, 55) sts*

Continue straight in Waffle Stitch as set until Waffle Stitch section measures 19 (20, 21, 21.5, 24, 24, 25.5, 28, 29) cm / 7½ (8, 8¼, 8½, 9½, 9½, 10, 11, 11½)" ending with a RS row.
Place rem 30 (32, 35, 38, 42, 45, 48, 52, 55) sts on waste yarn or stitch holder.

BACK

With RS facing, place the 87 (95, 103, 113, 123, 131, 139, 147, 159) held Back sts on larger 80 cm / 32" circular needle. Rejoin yarn and work back and forth in rows of Waffle Stitch as follows:
Row 1 (RS): K2, p1, [k1, p1] to last 2 sts, k2.
Row 2 (WS): Purl.
Repeat rows 1-2 until section measures 19 (20, 21, 21.5, 24, 24, 25.5, 28, 29) cm / 7½ (8, 8¼, 8½, 9½, 9½, 10, 11, 11½)" to match Front in length, ending with a WS row.
Next Row (RS): Patt 30 (32, 35, 38, 42, 45, 48, 52, 55) sts and place them on hold for right shoulder, cast off next 27 (31, 33, 37, 39, 41, 43, 43, 49) Back sts. Work in patt across 30 (32, 35, 38, 42, 45, 48, 52, 55) remaining left shoulder sts to end and place sts on hold.

JOIN SHOULDERS

Work a 3-needle cast off to join the shoulder as follows:
Place held front and back Right shoulder sts onto two different larger DPNs or circular needles. With RS together (so wrong sides are visible to you), join yarn at neck edge and work 3-needle cast off over front and back right shoulder sts. Repeat for Left shoulder sts.

BOTH VERSIONS - SLEEVES
(work both alike)

With RS facing, using larger needles suitable for working small circumferences in the round and yarn A if working Colour Block Version, beginning at bottom of armhole, pick up and k56 (60, 66, 70, 76, 82, 88, 96, 104) sts around

the armhole opening. Join for working in the round and PM to indicate beg of round.
Knit 2 rounds.
Dec round: K1, k2tog, k to 3 sts before marker, ssk, k1. *2 sts dec*
Work St st in the round (knit every round) until Sleeve measures 15.5 (15.5, 10, 10, 9, 7.5, 7.5, 7.5, 6.5) cm / 6 (6, 4, 4, 3½, 3, 3, 3, 2½)".
Rep Dec round as set on next and every foll 5th (5th, 5th, 4th, 4th, 4th, 3rd, 3rd, 3rd) round a further 6 (8, 11, 11, 14, 17, 18, 22, 26) times. *40 (40, 40, 44, 44, 44, 48, 48, 48) sts*

Work St st in the round until Sleeve measures 33 (34.5, 34.5, 34.5, 37, 38, 38, 38, 40.5) cm / 13 (13½, 13½, 13½, 14½, 15, 15, 15, 16)" or 5 cm / 2" less than desired final length.

Note: you can always lengthen and shorten sleeves too! If you want a shorter sleeve just work a shorter length here, for a longer sleeve keep going a little longer!

Cuff
Change to smaller needles.
Next round: Purl.
Work 2x2 Rib for 5 cm / 2".
Cast off loosely in 2x2 Rib pattern.

BOTH VERSIONS - NECKLINE
Using smaller needles suitable for working small circumferences in the round and yarn B if working Colour Block Version, with RS facing, starting at left shoulder, pick up and k19 (20, 21, 21, 21, 22, 22, 22, 23) sts down Front left neck, 14 (14, 14, 16, 16, 18, 18, 18, 20) from Front cast-off sts, 19 (20, 21, 21, 21, 22, 22, 22, 23) sts up Front right neck, and 28 (30, 32, 36, 38, 40, 42, 42, 48) sts across Back neck cast-off sts.
Join for working in the round and PM to indicate beg of round. *80 (84, 88, 94, 96, 102, 104, 104, 114) sts*
Next round: Purl across all sts, decreasing 0 (0, 0, 2, 0, 2, 4, 0, 2) sts evenly across the round. *80 (84, 88, 92, 96, 100, 100, 104, 112) sts*
This means spacing decreases - if applicable - at roughly equal intervals, using p2tog (see page 141 for p2tog tutorial).
Work 2x2 Rib for 2.5cm / 1".
Cast off loosely in rib.

FINISHING

Weave in all loose ends and block to measurements taking care not to overstretch the bottom rib.

a. Bust circumference: 96.5 (105.5, 114.5, 125.5, 136.5, 145.5, 155, 165, 178) cm / 38 (41½, 45, 49½, 54, 57½, 61, 65, 70)"

b. Length hem to underarm: 33 (33, 35.5, 35.5, 35.5, 38, 40.5, 43, 43) cm / 13 (13, 14, 14, 14, 15, 16, 17, 17)"

c. Neck circumference: 44.5 (46.5, 49, 51, 53, 55.5, 55.5, 57.5, 62) cm / 17½ (18½, 19¼, 20, 21, 21¾, 21¾, 22¾, 24½)"

d. Shoulder width: 17 (18, 19.5, 21.5, 23.5, 25, 27, 29, 31) cm / 6 ¾ (7, 7¾, 8½, 9¼, 10, 10¾, 11½, 12¼)"

e. Cuff circumference: 23 (23, 23, 25.5, 25.5, 25.5, 28, 28, 28) cm / 9 (9, 9, 10, 10, 10, 11, 11, 11)"

f. Upper arm circumference: 30.5 (33, 35.5, 38, 42, 44.5, 48, 53, 58.5) cm / 12 (13, 14, 15, 16½, 17½, 19, 21, 23)"

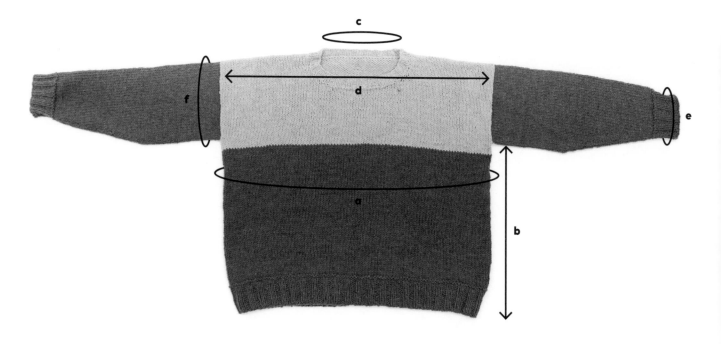

Putting Stitches on Hold (Using a Stitch Holder)

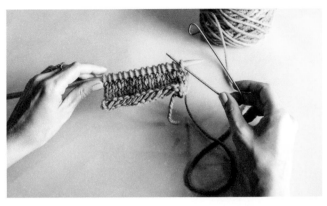

1. With your stitch holder in your right hand, insert into the first stitch on the left-hand needle purlwise. Slip this stitch off the needle and onto the holder.

2. Repeat for each stitch, transferring them from your left-hand needle across to the stitch holder.

3. Close the stitch holder to keep your stitches safe.

Putting Stitches on Hold (Using Scrap Yarn)

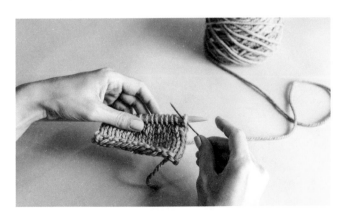

1. Thread your tapestry needle with scrap yarn (a smooth yarn is best for this as it is much easier to get your stitches back on your needles later). Insert your needle into the first stitch on the left-hand needle purlwise.

2. Slip this stitch off the left-hand needle and pass onto your tapestry needle, allowing it to slide down onto the scrap yarn. Repeat steps until you have slipped all the required stitches onto your scrap yarn.

Picking Up Stitches

1. Ready to pick up some stitches!

2. With the right side of your work facing you, hold one needle in your right hand. Insert the tip of the needle into the first stitch under both strands at the edge (to pick up this stitch).

3. Wrap yarn around needle and draw loop through - the same steps you use to knit a stitch.

4. Repeat steps 2 - 3, evenly pick up stitches along the edge of your work.

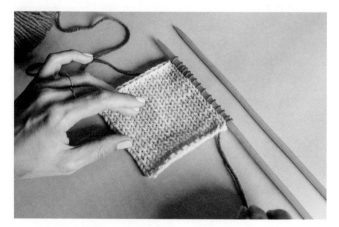

5. Here we've picked up 15 stitches.

6. You can now knit across these stitches as normal.

Three-Needle Cast Off

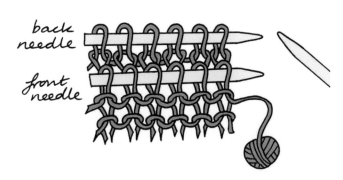

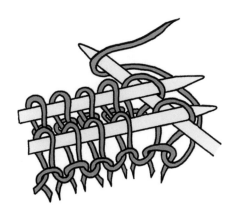

1. Begin with needles parallel and stitches at the tips. Use a DPN or spare needle to work the cast-off.

2. Insert the DPN knitwise through first stitch on front needle, then first stitch on back needle. Draw yarn through both stitches as you would for a knit stitch.

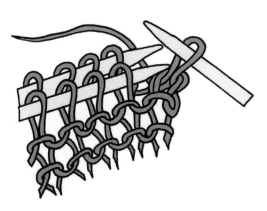

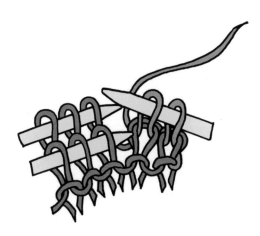

3. Draw wrapped loop through, allowing first stitch from front and back needle to drop off.

4. Repeat steps 2-3, two stitches on DPN.

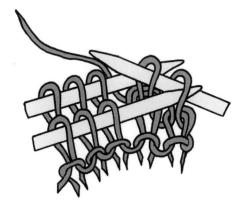

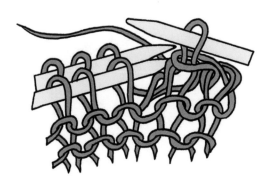

5. Use front needle to pick up first stitch on DPN and lift and leap-frog first stitch over the second stitch (like you would for a regular cast-off). Drop the picked-up stitch off the end of the DPN, removing left-hand needle from loop and making sure that second stitch remains on DPN.

6. One stitch cast off! Repeat steps 2-5 to cast off all stitches until one stitch remains. Finish last stitch as normal cast-off.

Knit How

M-A-D-E-L-I-N-E

Simple Lace Cowl

Project 8: Madeline

This cowl is perfect for autumn, when there's a chill in the air but it's not quite time to get the chunky knits out. The simple lace will help you master the basics of lace knitting, which is nothing more than knitting with decorative holes between your stitches (a bit like regular lace). To start with, you will want to carefully keep track of where you are in the sequence of rows that make the pattern. If you are working from the written instructions, you could use a row counter (a little gadget you can get from your LYS) or just keep a tally! After a while, you may get a feel for what's next as the repeat starts to become more intuitive. Lace knitting is one area where charts really help (in our opinion). So if you haven't tried them yet, we recommend you give them a go here!

Notes on Construction:
This cowl is knit flat as a rectangle and seamed short end to short end to form a loop.

Techniques You Need to Know:
- Casting on (see page 74)
- Knit stitch (see page 14)
- Purl stitch (see page 18)
- Casting off in pattern (see page 50)
- Reading from charts (see page 92)

Techniques Introduced:
- Yarn overs
- Reading from charts and boxed repeats

Bonus Info:
Lace knitting can be addictive. It's a lot of fun seeing the pattern emerge, and often you get a strong urge to just do one more row (and then just one more...). When it comes to knitting lace, blocking really is your BFF. Sometimes it can look unimpressive until it's blocked properly. Blocking helps open the lace up and reveal it in its true glory. We highly recommend knitting and blocking a swatch for this one so you can see the magic happen before you get started on the main thing!

Top Tips!
Chart Repeats

Keep track of which row of the chart you are on in lace knitting by marking your chart with a sticky note or decorative washi tape. If you don't already know washi tape, it's a low-tack Japanese paper tape that you can find in most stationery and craft shops.

When you look at the chart for this pattern you'll notice a box in a different colour around the section of the rows which should be repeated. This works in the same way as bracketed repeats in written patterns: repeat the stitches inside the box for the row you are working as many times as instructed. Then move on to the next stitch after the boxed repeat.

Yarn Overs

This cowl uses yarn overs to create decorative lacey holes. As well as making a little (intentional) hole in your knitting, a yarn over creates a new stitch. For this pattern we don't want to increase the stitch count so in order to stop your cowl getting wider and wider, each yarn over is paired with a decrease to keep your number of stitches nice and stable.

Pattern 8: Madeline

One size: 20 cm / 8" deep x 135 cm / 53" circumference
Yarn: Madelinetosh Tosh DK (DK weight; 100% Merino wool; 206 m / 225 yds per 100 g skein)
Shade: Fog (green); 3 skeins
OR Scout (pink); 3 skeins
Gauge: 22 sts & 24 rows = 10 cm / 4" over lace pattern on 5 mm needles, unstretched, after blocking.
Needles: 5 mm / US 8 knitting needles
Always use a needle size that will result in the correct gauge after blocking.
Notions: 9 stitch markers (optional), tapestry needle

PATTERN BEGINS
Using the long-tail method, cast on 48 sts.
Set-up row (WS): P3, [k2, p3] to end.

LACE PATTERN
Starting with a RS row 1, commence lace pattern reading from the Chart or Written Instructions below, and working the main boxed repeat 8 times.
Note: You may find it helpful to place markers between each repeat of the Lace Pattern.
WRITTEN INSTRUCTIONS FOR CHART
Row 1 (RS): K3, p2, [k2tog, yo, k1, p2] 8 times, k3.
Row 2 (WS): P3, [k2, p3] to end.
Row 3: K3, p2, [k1, yo, ssk, p2] 8 times, k3.
Row 4 (WS): As row 2.
Rep rows 1-4 of lace pattern until scarf measures 135 cm / 53" from cast-on edge, ending after row 4.

Cast off in [k3, p2] rib.

FINISHING
Seam the two short ends together using mattress stitch and weave in ends. Block to measurements.

a. Depth: 20 cm / 8"
b. Circumference: 135 cm / 53"

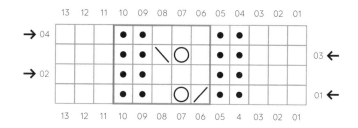

Key

	RS: knit / WS: purl
●	RS: purl / WS: knit
○	yo
/	k2tog
\	ssk
	repeat

Yarn Over

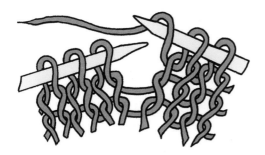

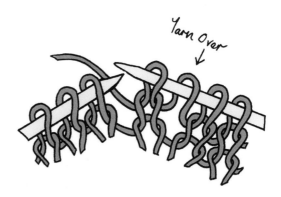

1. Move yarn from front between your needles as if to purl, and then to back, catching it over your right-hand needle as shown.

2. This strand should stay over the needle as you continue to work the following stitches. Your yarn over is essentially a brand new stitch! Note that the yarn sits with left leg behind and right leg in front of the needle as with you other stitches.

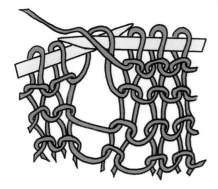

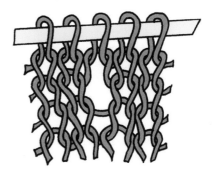

3. When you reach your yarn over on the next row, work it as if it's a stitch. (shown here is WS of stocking stitch).

4. The finished Yarn Over leaves a cute little hole in your work, like a knitted polka dot!

Knit How

FRANKIE

First Cardigan

A wardrobe staple, the classic cardi is the ultimate transformational item. Think about it. Weather can't make its mind up? Throw on your cardigan. Your outfit needs a splash of colour? That's right, it's cardigan time. There are very few situations where this cosy cardi won't be welcome, you might even find you need one in every colour. Plus, now that you've mastered so many techniques, it's time to put them together. Of course, we're still here to guide you through the new steps as you progress with circular needles. Think of how far you've come from those first few stitches... can you knit this? We say yes you cardi-CAN!

Notes on Construction:

The cardigan is worked from the neckline down, with the yoke and body worked flat on circular needles and the sleeves worked in the round. The cardigan features alternating bands of garter stitch and stocking stitch. Then the neck, hem, and cuffs are all worked in garter stitch.

Techniques You Need to Know:

- Casting on (see page 12)
- Knit stitch (see page 14)
- Purl stitch (see page 18)
- Knitting small circumferences in the round (DPNs or Magic Loop) (see page 64-67)
- Ssk and k2tog decreases (see page 76)
- M1L and M1R increases (see page 103 & 104)
- Picking up stitches (see page 105)
- Putting stitches on hold (see page 115)

Techniques Introduced:

- Knitting flat on circular needles
- Raglan shaping
- Backwards loop cast-on

Bonus Info:

The type of shaping you will be working for this cardigan is known as 'raglan'. Raglan refers to a way in which the sleeves and body of a jumper or cardigan are joined. You'll see diagonal lines from the neck to the armpit - this is the raglan! For this cardigan, your increases create the raglan shaping.

Top Tips!
Knitting Flat on Circular Needles

As you may remember from Project 4 (cuffs), it's possible to knit flat (in rows) on circular needles. In fact, we always use circular needles to knit flat, for lots of reasons! For us, the pros are that you can't lose one of your needles, and that stitches are less likely to slip off the end of your needles when you don't want them to. Of course, there's no problem using straight needles for most flat knitting... except when you need to hold a large number of stitches at one time. For this cardigan, you will be working body and sleeve stitches at once. This means a lot of stitches, so circular needles will definitely make your life easier!

Working Two Sets of Instructions at the Same Time

Often in more complex patterns, you will be asked to work two sets of instructions 'at the same time'. This might be a set of increases or decreases which are run parallel to an established stitch pattern, like stripes, for example. This can be quite tricky as they can have different length repeats, such as increasing every 5 rows whilst changing stripes every 8 rows. A clever way to keep track of your instructions is to draw out a little table with your row numbers on one side, and the relevant instruction on the other. This way you know that when you get to a certain row, you may work one particular instruction, or both, and so on. Sometimes you will work both sets of instructions on the same row. This is where this table can come in handy to remind you where you are and what is happening on any given row.

Pattern 9: Frankie

Sizes: 1 (2, 3, 4, 5, 6, 7)

Finished bust measurement (open at front): 86.5 (95.5, 103, 112.5, 124.5, 131.5, 138) cm / 34 (37½, 40½, 44¼, 49, 51¾, 54¼)" – to be worn with 5 - 10 cm / 2-4" positive ease.
Ayesha has 86 cm / 34" bust, stands 166 cm / 5'5" tall and is wearing a size 3.
Roshni has 81 cm / 32" bust, stands 173 cm / 5'8" tall and is wearing a size 2.
Yarn (orange version, shown on Ayesha): Green Mountain Spinnery Mountain Mohair (worsted weight; 70% wool, 30% Yearling Mohair; 128 m / 140 yds per 58 g skein)
Shade: Day Lily; 4 (5, 5, 6, 7, 8, 9) skeins
Yarn (grey version, shown on Roshni): Julie Asselin Nurtured (worsted weight; 100% fine wool (Rambouillet, Targhee, and Merino); 118 m / 130 yds per 56 g skein)
Shade: Courtepointe; 5 (6, 6, 7, 8, 9, 10) skeins

Gauge: 14 sts & 25 rows = 10 cm / 4" over stocking stitch on 5.5 mm needles after blocking.
Needles: 5.5 mm / US 9 circular needle, 80 cm / 32" length **AND** DPNs or circular needle for working sleeves in the round. Always use a needle size that will result in the correct gauge after blocking.
Notions: 10 stitch markers (5 of type A, 5 of type B), stitch holders or waste yarn, tapestry needle

PATTERN BEGINS
YOKE
Using the long-tail method, cast on 65 (65, 68, 73, 78, 81, 82) sts. Knit 7 rows.
Next row (WS): K5, PM A, k1, PM A, k1, PM B, k12 (12, 12, 14, 16, 17, 17), PM B, k1, PM A, k25 (25, 28, 29, 30, 31, 32), PM A, k1, PM B, k12 (12, 12, 14, 16, 17, 17), PM B, k1, PM A, k1, PM A, k5.

Set-up row (RS): K5, SM A, k1, M1R, SM A, k1, SM B, M1L, k to marker, M1R, SM B, k1, SM A, M1L, k to marker, M1R, SM A, k1, SM B, M1L, k to marker, M1R, SM B, k1, SM A, M1L, k1, SM A, k5.
73 (73, 76, 81, 86, 89, 90) sts
Next row (WS): K5, p to last 5 sts slipping markers as you pass them, k5.

Note: The Sleeves and Body increase at slightly different rates, using two different coloured stitch markers will help identify which is which. Read the following section through carefully as you will be working multiple instructions **AT THE SAME TIME.**

Maintaining garter stitch front bands over first and last 5 sts of every row throughout, continue in St st and work Raglan increases as foll:

Body raglan increases
Body inc row (RS): K5, SM A, k to marker, M1R, SM A, k1, SM B, k to marker, SM B, k1, SM A, M1L, k to marker, M1R, SM A, k1, SM B, k to marker, SM B, k1, SM A, M1L, k to marker, SM A, k5.
2 sts inc on Back, 1 st inc each Front

Repeat Body inc row every 2nd row a further 8 (11, 13, 19, 24, 27, 29) times, then every 4th row 6 (6, 6, 3, 1, 0, 0) times. *57 (63, 70, 77, 84, 89, 94) sts for Back, 17 (20, 22, 25, 28, 30, 32) sts each Front (excluding raglan sts and front bands)*

AT THE SAME TIME, work **Sleeve raglan increases:**
Sleeve inc row (RS): K5, SM A, k to marker, SM A, k1, SM B, M1L, k to marker, M1R, SM B, k1, SM A, k to marker, SM A, k1, SM B, M1L, k to marker, M1R, SM B, k1, SM A, k to marker, SM A, k5.
2 sts inc on each Sleeve

Repeat Sleeve inc row every 2nd row a further 6 (3, 3, 7, 10, 15, 15) times, then every 4th row 7 (10, 11, 9, 8, 6, 7) times. *42 (42, 44, 50, 56, 63, 65) sts for each Sleeve*

AT THE SAME TIME
When 42 (48, 52, 52, 54, 56, 60) rows have been worked from cast-on edge, ending with a WS row, work next 10 rows in garter st (see page 24 for a reminder of how to work garter st), including Body and Sleeve raglan increases if necessary.

When raglan shaping and garter st band have been completed, there will be 189 (201, 216, 241, 266, 289, 302) sts total: 5 sts each front band, 4 raglan sts, 42 (42, 44, 50, 56, 63, 65) sts each Sleeve, 57 (63, 70, 77, 84, 89, 94) sts for Back, 17 (20, 22, 25, 28, 30, 32) sts each Front

Divide Body and Sleeves

Maintaining 5-st garter bands at Fronts, beg with a RS knit row, work 4 rows in St st.

Next row (RS): Removing markers as you pass them, knit 23 (26, 28, 31, 34, 36, 38) sts across Right Front, place next 42 (42, 44, 50, 56, 63, 65) sts on waste yarn for Right Sleeve, using Backwards Loop method cast on 7 (7, 7, 7, 9, 9, 9) sts

for underarm gusset, knit 59 (65, 72, 79, 86, 91, 96) sts across Back, place next 42 (42, 44, 50, 56, 63, 65) sts on waste yarn for Left Sleeve, using Backwards Loop method cast on 7 (7, 7, 7, 9, 9, 9) sts for underarm gusset, k to end. *119 (131, 142, 155, 172, 181, 190) Body sts*

LOWER BODY

Maintaining 5 st garter bands at Fronts, continue working flat on Body sts only as follows:
Beg with a purl row, work 8 rows in St st.
Work 10 rows in Garter st.
Beg with a purl row, work 14 rows in St st.
Work 13 (13, 13, 19, 19, 23, 23) rows in Garter st.
Cast off.

SLEEVES (both alike)

Using needles suitable for working small circumferences in the round, with RS facing and working from right to left, pick up and k8 (8, 8, 8, 10, 10, 10) sts across underarm cast-on sts, knit across 42 (42, 44, 50, 56, 63, 65) held sleeve sts, join for working in the round, ssk, k3 (3, 3, 3, 4, 4, 4), PM to indicate beg of round. *49 (49, 51, 57, 65, 72, 74) sts*

Note: Read the foll section carefully before beginning as sleeve decreases and textured sequence are worked **AT THE SAME TIME.**

Work texture sequence as follows:
Work 7 rounds in St st.
Work 9 rounds Garter st (purl 1 round, knit 1 round), beg with a purl round.
Work 13 rounds St st.
Rep last 22 rounds a further 3 times.
Work even in Garter st to end of sleeve.

AT THE SAME TIME shape sleeves as follows:
Work in pattern for 5 rounds.
Dec round: K2tog, work in pattern to last 2 sts, ssk. *2 sts dec*
Repeat Dec round every 10th (10th, 10th, 8th, 6th, 6th, 6th) round 0 (4, 0, 5, 12, 6, 4) times, then every 8th (8th, 8th, 6th, 4th, 4th, 4th) round 11 (6, 11, 8, 4, 13, 16) times. *25 (27, 27, 29, 31, 32, 32) sts*

Work straight in pattern until Sleeve measures 42.5 (43, 44, 44, 44.5, 44.5, 46) cm / 16¾ (17, 17¼, 17¼, 17½, 17½, 18)".

FINISHING

Weave in ends. Soak in lukewarm soapy water, squeeze out excess water without wringing, block flat to measurements and allow to dry.

a. Bust measurement (open): 86.5 (95.5, 103, 112.5, 124.5, 131.5, 138) cm / 34 (37½, 40½, 44¼, 49, 51¾, 54¼)

b. Yoke length (excluding neckband): 18.5 (20.5, 22, 22, 23, 24, 25.5) cm / 7¼ (8, 8¾, 8¾, 9, 9½, 10)"

c. Length (underarm to hem): 20.5 (20.5, 20.5, 23, 23, 24, 24) cm / 8 (8, 8, 9, 9, 9½, 9½)"

d. Neck width: 18 (18, 20.5, 21, 21.5, 22.5, 23) cm / 7 (7, 8, 8¼, 8½, 8¾, 9)"

e. Upper arm circumference: 35.5 (35.5, 37, 41, 47, 52, 53.5) cm / 14 (14, 14½, 16¼, 18½, 20½, 21)"

f. Cuff circumference: 18 (19.5, 19.5, 21, 22.5, 23, 23) cm / 7 (7¾, 7¾, 8¼, 8¾, 9, 9)"

g. Sleeve length: 42.5 (43, 44, 44, 44.5, 44.5, 46) cm / 16¾ (17, 17¼, 17¼, 17½, 17½, 18)"

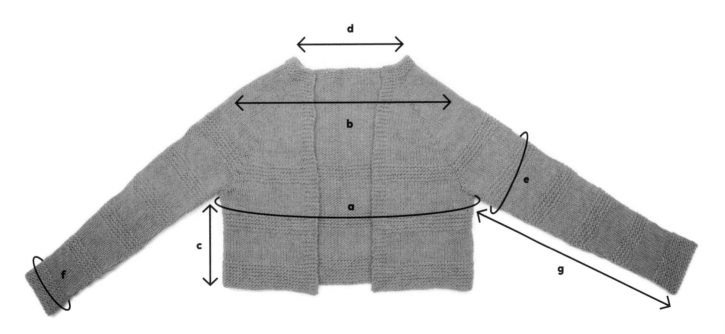

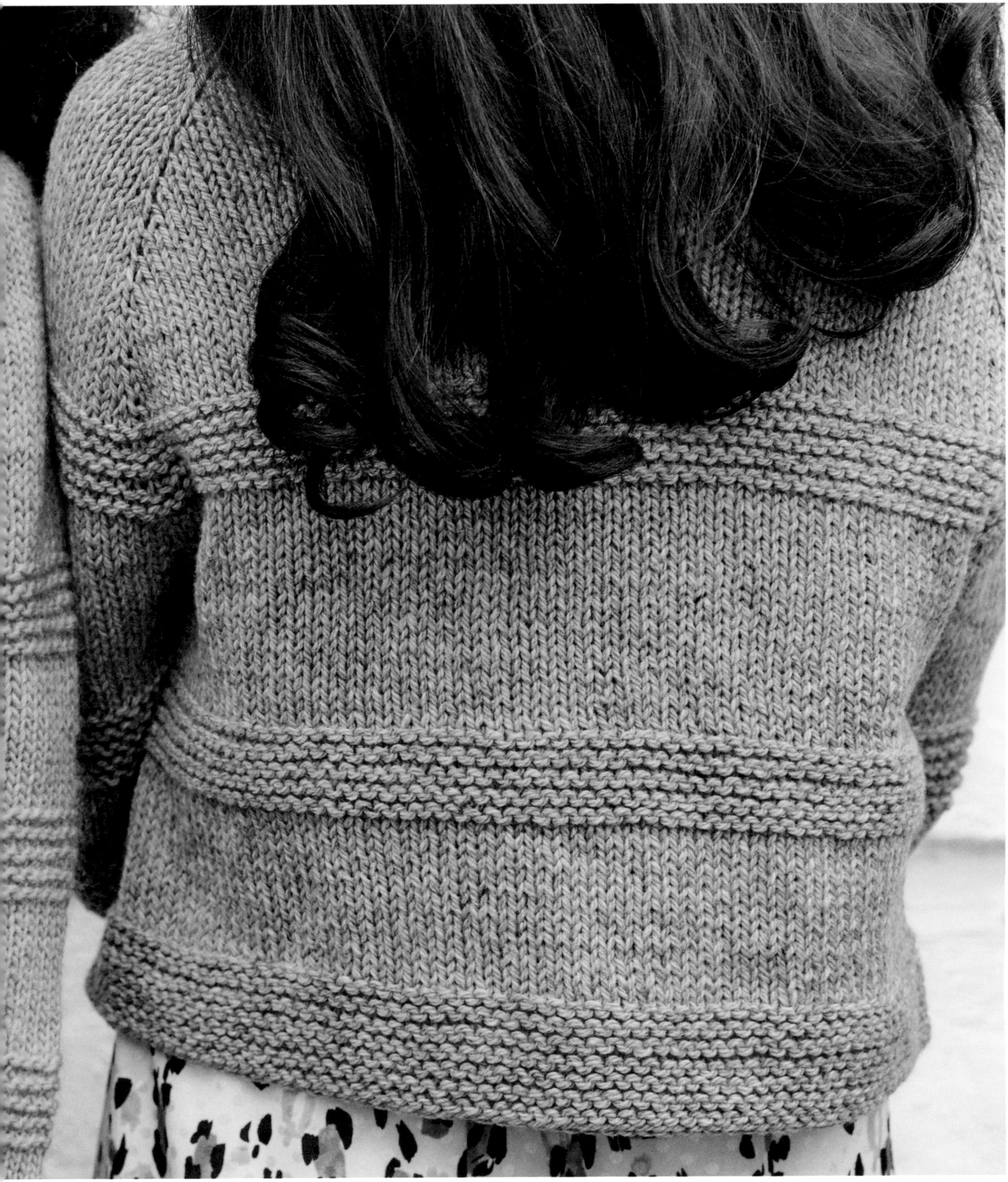

Backwards Loop Cast-On

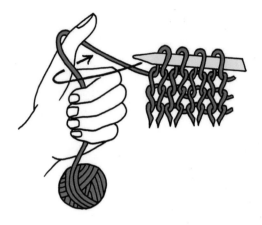

1. Loop your working yarn around your thumb and grasp it as shown. Your right needle goes under the yarn closest to you, in the direction shown by the arrow.

2. Your yarn will now be looped over the needle, as shown.

3. Drop the yarn from your thumb so that it's now sitting on your needle, as shown. You can tighten your stitch by pulling the yarn in the direction indicated by the arrow.

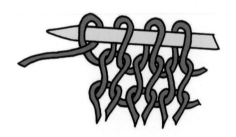

4. Your new stitch should be snug on the needle as shown, but not too tight.

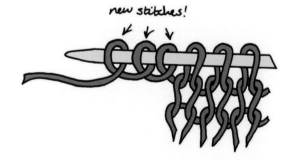

5. Repeat steps 1-3 until you have created the required number of new stitches.

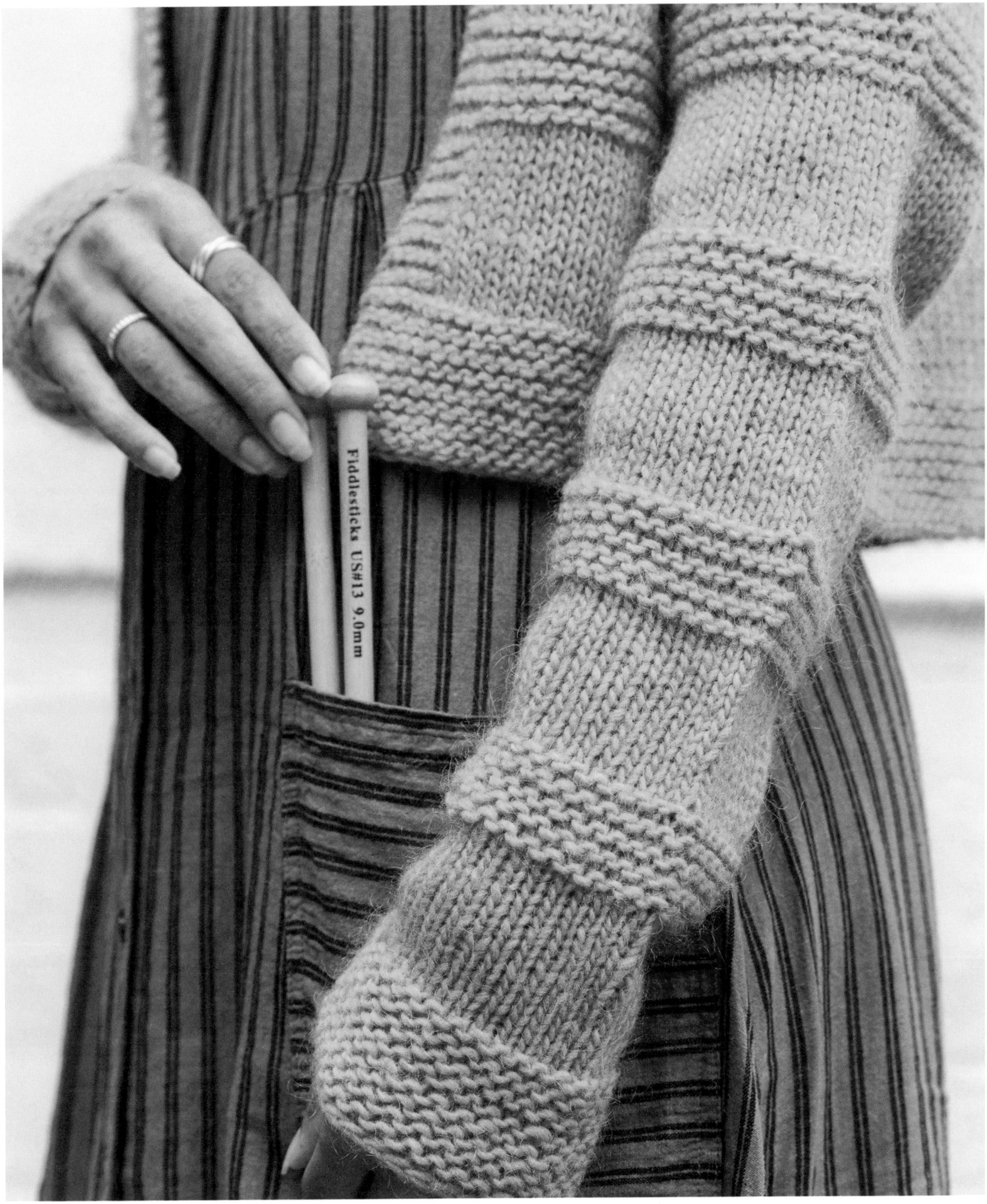
Fiddlesticks US#13 9.0mm

R-A-C-H-E-L

Simple Bed Socks

Project 10: Rachel

It might seem odd to make something that will likely only ever be worn at home or hidden in a shoe. But we promise you that handmade socks are one of the greatest pleasures that knitting can bring. There is no sock more comfortable and it's hard to beat wool for keeping toes warm. These socks are designed to be worn around the house and to bed in the cold months. Knit in a relatively thick yarn, these socks knit up in a snap while guiding you through the fundamentals of how socks work. Mostly they are knit in the round but the real magic happens when you turn the heel. It's difficult to explain a heel turn in the abstract so we fully recommend following the instructions without studying them too much beforehand. Be careful who you give your handmade socks to - they are addictive and you may be fielding many requests for your handiwork.

Notes on Construction:

These socks are knit 'top-down', which means you start at the ribbing around the leg and work downwards. You then turn your heel, and work the foot, finally decreasing for the toe.

Techniques You Need to Know:

- Long-tail cast-on (see page 74)
- Knit stitch (see page 14)
- Purl stitch (see page 18)
- Knitting small circumferences in the round (DPNs or Magic Loop, see page 64-67)
- Ssk and K2tog decreases (see page 76)
- 2x2 ribbing (see page 72)

Techniques Introduced:

- Turning a heel (short rows)
- Grafting (aka Kitchener stitch)
- Decreasing (p2tog)

Bonus Info:

There are many, many ways to turn a heel. This pattern uses a garden-variety, tried and tested technique. It also happens to be a favourite here at Pom Pom. It's simple and effective and makes very comfy socks! If you find your interest piqued in the engineering of socks after making these, then do try out other methods as soon as you feel ready. You may only try some heel techniques once, but oh boy will you learn!

As a side note, making a heel turn is one of the knitting techniques that really brings home how technically impressive knitting can be; it's the original 3D printing.

Top Tip! Short Rows

Put simply, short rows are partially worked rows. Imagine you have 10 sts, and you knit 5 of them, and then turn your work before the end of the row, then work back over that first 5. That's a short row! There are a lot of ways to work short rows and a lot of reasons to use them. We find the kind of short rows worked in this type of heel are the easiest, and think they make a great introduction to the concept. Short rows help to create extra fabric in just one area, for example a heel.

Pattern 10: Rachel

Sizes: 1 (2, 3, 4)
Foot circumference: 18.5 (20.5, 23.5, 25.5) cm / 7¼ (8, 9¼, 10)"
Foot length: Adjust to fit
Yarn: Coop Knits Socks Yeah! DK (DK weight; 75% superwash Merino wool, 25% nylon; 112 m / 122 yds per 50 g ball)
Shades:
A: Tyburn (green); 1 (1, 1, 1) skeins
B: Tartarus (dark grey); 2 (2, 2, 3) skeins
C: Minos (light grey); 1 (1, 1, 1) skeins
OR
A: Pigeon (grey);1 (1, 1, 1) skeins
B: Moselle (dark red); 2 (2, 2, 3) skeins
C: Ammolite (coral); 1 (1, 1, 1) skeins
Gauge: 24 sts & 28 rows = 10 cm / 4" over stocking stitch worked in the round on 3.75 mm needles after blocking
Needles: 3.75 mm / US 5 circular needle, 80 cm / 32" length for working Magic Loop **OR** a set of four DPNs – pattern includes instructions for both types of needle.
Always use a needle size that will result in the correct gauge after blocking.
Notions: 3 stitch markers, tapestry needle

PATTERN BEGINS
(make 2 alike)
CUFF
Using yarn A and the long-tail method, cast on 44 (48, 56, 60) sts. Join for working in the round, being careful not to twist. PM to indicate beg of round.
Distribute the sts evenly over the needles – if you are working Magic Loop technique, split the sts in half with 22 (24, 28, 30) on each needle. For DPNs, distribute sts as follows: 16 (16, 20, 20) sts on needle 1, 16 (16, 20, 20) sts on needle 2, 12 (16, 16, 20) sts on needle 3 and use needle 4 to knit with.

Round 1: [K2, p2] to end of round.
Round 1 sets 2x2 rib.
Work in 2x2 rib for a further 11 rounds, or until piece measures 3.5 cm / 1½" from cast-on edge.
Cut yarn A leaving a 15 cm / 6" tail to weave in later.

LEG
Next Round: Join yarn B and knit to end of round.
Work St st in the round (knit every round) until Leg measures 14 (14, 15.5, 15.5) cm / 5½ (5½, 6, 6)" from cast-on edge.
If you would like longer or shorter socks you can adjust the length here but remember you may need more yarn!

HEEL FLAP
Set-up row (RS): K11 (12, 14, 15) sts, turn your work so that the WS (purl side) is facing.
Set-up row (WS): Sl1 pwise wyif, p21 (23, 27, 29), removing beg of round marker as you pass it.
These 22 (24, 28, 30) sts just worked are your heel stitches, you will be working back and forth on them to form the heel flap.
The remaining 22 (24, 28, 30) stitches will be worked later for the instep. If you are using Magic Loop the instep sts can be left on the cable while you work the heel sts. If you are using DPNs leave the instep sts on two DPNs while you work the rows with the other 2.

Row 1 (RS): Sl1 pwise wyib, k to end.
Row 2 (WS): Sl1 pwise wyif, p to end.
Rep rows 1 and 2 a further 8 (9, 11, 13) times – 9 (10, 12, 14) chain stitches along each selvedge edge of the heel flap.

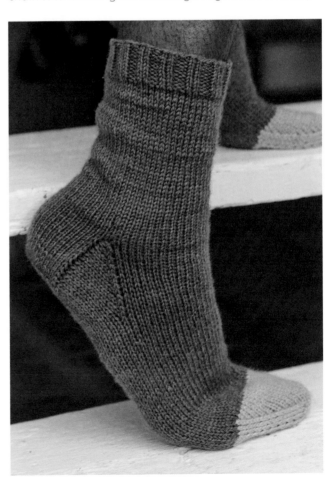

Pattern 10: Rachel

TURN HEEL

Working in short rows, shape the heel as follows:

Row 1 (RS): K13 (14, 17, 19), ssk, k1, turn work. *1 st dec*

Row 2 (WS): Sl1 pwise wyif, p5 (5, 7, 9), p2tog, p1, turn. *1 st dec*

Row 3: Sl1 pwise wyib, k to 1 st before gap formed on previous row, ssk (one stitch from each side of gap), k1, turn. *1 st dec*

Row 4: Sl1 pwise wyif, p to 1 st before gap formed on previous row, p2tog (one stitch from each side of gap), p1, turn. *1 st dec*

Rep rows 3 and 4 a further 2 (2, 3, 3) times.

Next row: K to last 2 sts, ssk, turn.

Next row: P to last 2 sts, p2tog, turn.

All heel stitches have been worked and 12 (14, 16, 18) heel sts remain.

SHAPE GUSSET

Note: Instructions are different depending on whether you are working on DPNs or Magic Loop.

For DPNS only:

Set-up round: Using needle 1, sl1, k11 (13, 15, 17) heel sts, pick up and k1 st in each of the 9 (10, 12, 14) slipped sts along the side of the heel flap, pick up and k1 st between the heel flap and instep to close the gap; using needle 2 knit across the 22 (24, 28, 30) held instep sts; using needle 3 pick up and k1 st between the heel flap and instep to close the gap, pick up and k1 st in each of the 9 (10, 12, 14) slipped sts along the other side of the heel flap, k6 (7, 8, 9) sts from needle 1.

PM for new beginning of round at centre of the heel. *54 (60, 70, 78) sts total; 16 (18, 21, 24) sts each on needles 1 and 3; 22 (24, 28, 30) instep sts on needle 2*

Work gusset decreases as follows:

Round 1 (Dec round): On needle 1, k to last 3 sts, k2tog, k1; on needle 2, work St st as set; on needle 3, k1, ssk, k to end. *2 sts dec*

Round 2: Knit.

Rep rounds 1 - 2 a further 4 (5, 6, 8) times. *44 (48, 56, 60) sts*

For Magic Loop only:

Set-up round: Using needle 1, sl1, k11 (13, 15, 17) heel sts, pick up and k1 st in each of the 9 (10, 12, 14) slipped sts along the side of the heel flap, pick up and k1 st between the heel flap and instep to close the gap, knit across 11 (12, 14, 15) held instep sts; using needle 2 knit across 11 (12, 14, 15) held instep sts, pick up and k1 st between the heel flap and instep to close the gap, pick up and k1 st in each of the 9 (10, 12, 14) slipped sts along the other side of the heel flap, k6 (7, 8, 9) sts from needle 1. PM for new beginning of round at centre of the heel. *54 (60, 70, 78) sts total; 27 (30, 35, 39) on each needle*

Round 1 (Dec Set-up): On needle 1, k14 (16, 19, 22), k2tog, PM, k to end; on needle 2, k11 (12, 14, 15), PM, ssk, k to end. *52 (58, 68, 76) sts*

Round 2: Knit.

Round 3 (Dec round): On needle 1, k to 2 sts before marker, k2tog, SM, k to end; on needle 2, k to marker, SM, ssk, k to end. *2 sts dec*

Round 4: Knit.

Rep rounds 3 - 4 a further 3 (4, 5, 7) times. *44 (48, 56, 60) sts total; 22 (24, 28, 30) on each needle*

BOTH METHODS AGAIN:
FOOT

Removing markers as you come to them, work St st in the round (knit every round) until foot measures 5 cm / 2" less than total length desired.

TOE
For DPNs only:

Next round: Break yarn B leaving a 15 cm / 6" tail to weave in later. Join yarn C, k to end.

Round 1: Knit

Round 2 (Dec round): On needle 1, k to last 3 sts, k2tog, k1; on needle 2: k1, ssk, k to last 3 sts, k2tog, k1; on needle 3; k1, ssk, k to end. *4 sts dec*

Round 3: Knit.
Rep rounds 2 - 3 a further 4 (5, 6, 7) times. *24 (24, 28, 28) sts*
Rep round 2 only a further 4 times. *8 (8, 12, 12) sts*
K2 (2, 3, 3) sts from Needle 1 onto the end of Needle 3. *4 (4, 6, 6) sts each on two needles*

For Magic Loop only:
K11 (12, 14, 15) sts, PM for new beg of round. Adjust sts so that 22 (24, 28, 30) instep sts are on Needle 1 and 22 (24, 28, 30) sole sts are on Needle 2. As you begin the next round, you will slip beg of round marker first before knitting across the sts on needle 1, meaning beg of round marker will sit on the cord between needles. This ensures stitches are divided evenly before beginning decreases.

Next round: Break yarn B leaving a 15 cm / 6" tail to weave in later. Join yarn C, k to end.
Round 1: Knit.
Round 2 (Dec round): On Needle 1, *k1, ssk, k to last 3 sts, k2tog, k1; rep from * once on Needle 2. *4 sts dec*

Round 3: Knit.
Rep rounds 2 - 3 a further 4 (5, 6, 7) times. *24 (24, 28, 28) sts*
Rep round 2 **only** 4 times. *8 (8, 12, 12) sts*
Ensure you have 4 (4, 6, 6) sts on each needle.

FINISHING
Graft the toe sts using Kitchener stitch (see page 140) OR thread yarn through rem sts and pull to tighten.
Weave in all loose ends and block to measurements.

a. Foot circumference: 18.5 (20.5, 23.5, 25.5) cm / 7¼ (8, 9¼, 10)"
b. Foot length: Adjustable (see below)

Measuring Feet

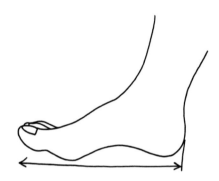

1. To work out the length of your foot, measure from your heel to your longest toe.

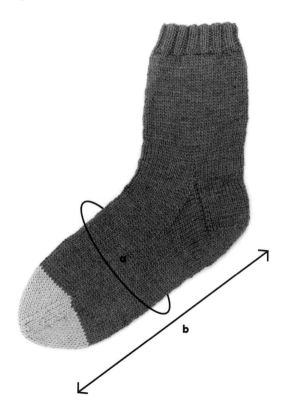

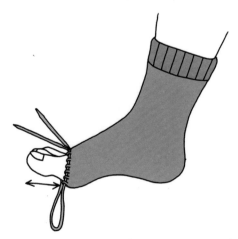

2. The magic of socks is that you can try them on as you go to make sure the length is correct. Carefully ease them onto your foot and measure from the toe to ensure the correct distance is left to knit your toe decreases.

Grafting (a.k.a Kitchener stitch)

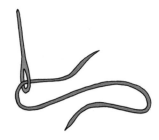

1. Thread your tapestry needle with working yarn or other length of yarn.

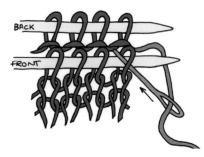

2. Arrange needles so they are parallel, with stitches at tip. Insert tapestry needle purlwise into first stitch on front needle and pull yarn through, leaving stitch on front needle.

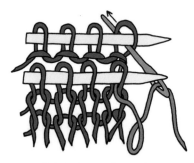

3. Insert tapestry needle knitwise into first stitch on back needle. Pull yarn through, leaving stitch on back needle.

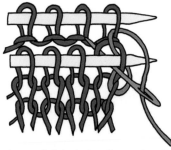

4. Insert tapestry needle knitwise into first stitch on front needle.

5. Slip this stitch off front needle. Enter next stitch purlwise and pull yarn through, leaving stitch on the front needle.

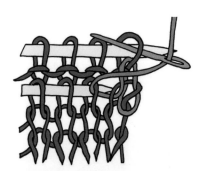

6. Insert tapestry needle purlwise into first stitch on back needle.

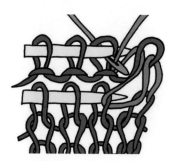

7. Slip this stitch off back needle. Enter next stitch knitwise and pull yarn through, leaving this stitch on back needle.

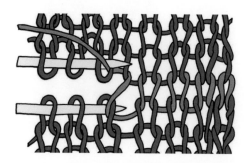

8. Repeat steps 4-7, weaving stitches together and adjusting your tension as you go. Continue until you have one stitch left on each needle. To finish, insert tapestry needle knitwise into stitch on front needle and slip off. Then insert tapestry needle purlwise into stitch on back needle and slip off. Adjust tension and weave in ends.

Purl Two Together - P2tog

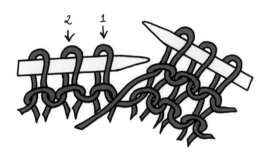

1. This method of decreasing uses all the same actions as a standard purl stitch, except that the first and second stitch are worked together.

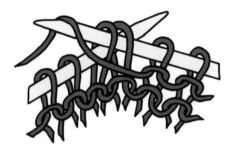

2. Insert right-hand needle into these two stitches like a purl stitch. First enter the right-hand side of first stitch, then through the second. Wrap yarn just like a purl stitch.

3. Draw the wrapped yarn through and drop two stitches off left-hand needle.

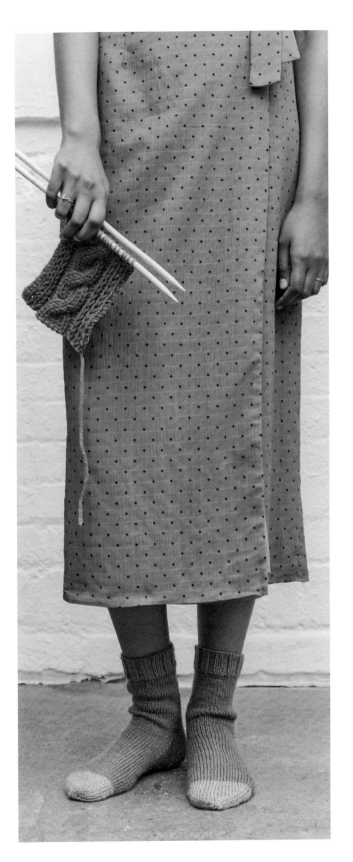

Part 3

FIXING MISTAKES AND LOVING YOUR MAKES

FIXING STUFF

One thing that we can guarantee in your knitting journey is that every project will involve you making a mistake. We would be shocked to hear about even a simple scarf that didn't need a stitch or two fixed at some point. So no need to let a dropped stitch or a misplaced purl get you down.

Mistakes aren't unique to beginners; even the most experienced knitters make mistakes. One of the wisest teachers we know likes to tell her students that the sign of a great knitter is not that they never make mistakes but that they can fix all their mistakes. The more mistakes you make, the better you'll get at fixing them!

Twisted Stitches

A common mistake beginners often run into is twisting stitches. This means that the left 'leg' of your stitch is oriented to the front of your needle. Unless specifically noted, the RIGHT leg of your stitch should be oriented to the front of your needle. Twisted stitches often look a little wonky and are tighter than correctly oriented stitches, making it more difficult to knit. If you find that every single one of your stitches is twisted, it's very likely that you are wrapping your working yarn around the needle in the wrong direction. The yarn should always be wrapped *anti-clockwise*. If it looks like you've just twisted a stitch or two, follow these steps to fix them.

Fixing Twisted Stitches - Quick

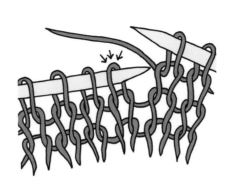

1. Identify the twisted stitch (shown here with the arrows).

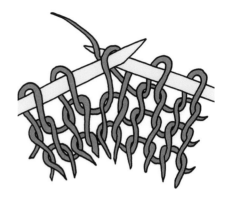

2. Insert your right-hand needle into the back of the stitch and knit it. The stitch is now untwisted!

Fixing Twisted Stitches - Slow and Steady

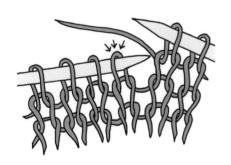

1. Identify the twisted stitch (shown here with arrows).

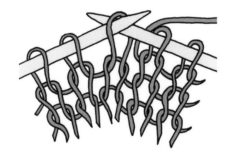

2. Insert right-hand needle into back of stitch.

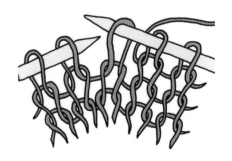

3. Slip left-hand needle out of stitch, so that it now sits on right-hand needle.

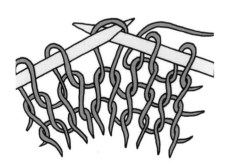

4. Return stitch to correct position on left-hand needle by inserting left-hand needle into stitch, as shown.

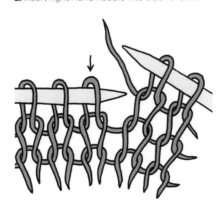

5. Slip right-hand needle out - stitch now sits in correct position on left-hand needle.

Dropped Stitches

One of the most common mistakes that beginners make is dropping a stitch. This means that a stitch falls off your needle and unravels a bit. The more slippery your yarn is, the more likely it is to drop, which is why we usually recommend wool to beginners. Even wool stitches can drop though, so here's what you need to do if (or, more likely, when!) this happens to you.

How to Pick Up a Dropped Knit Stitch

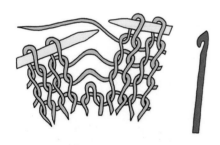

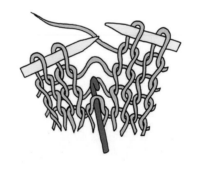

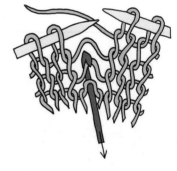

1. Here a stitch has dropped two rows. Each strand above the dropped loop is a row. To rescue it, use a crochet hook roughly the same size as the needles you are knitting with.

2. Insert crochet hook into dropped stitch from front to back.

3. Hook first strand above dropped stitch, draw through loop on crochet hook from back to front.

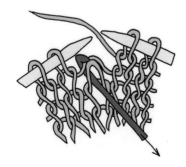

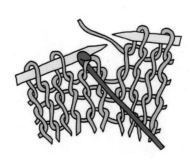

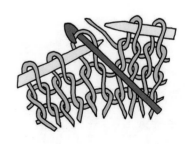

4. Repeat steps 2-3.

5. Here the two strands have been picked up and the dropped stitch has been rescued!

6. To finish, place stitch onto left-hand needle ensuring stitch is not twisted. Remove crochet hook.

How to Pick Up a Dropped Purl Stitch

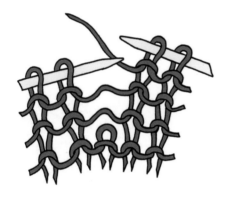

1. Here a stitch has dropped two rows. Each strand above the dropped loop is a row. To rescue it, use a crochet hook roughly the same size as the needles you are knitting with.

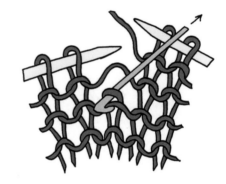

2. Insert crochet hook into dropped stitch from back to front. Gently lift the dropped stitch and catch the first strand above it, then draw the strand through the loop on the hook from front to back.

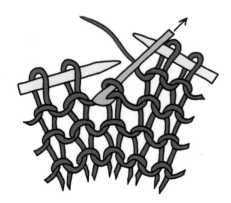

3. Repeat step 2 for second strand.

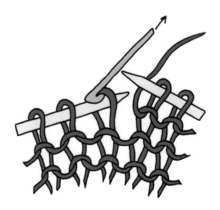

4. To finish, place stitch onto left-hand needle, ensuring stitch is not twisted. Remove crochet hook.

Tinking

You might find yourself happily knitting along when you notice a mistake that's been made a few stitches or even many rows back. Although this can be a common problem for beginners, it's not uncommon for experienced knitters either. Luckily it doesn't mean all is lost! When a mistake has been made on your previous stitch, or just a few stitches back, you can simply unpick those stitches and re-work them. Knitters like to call this 'tinking' because tink is knit spelled backwards and using this technique is basically reversing the knitting process. These drawings show 'tinking' worked on knit stitches but you can also unpick purl stitches in the same way.

<u>Unpicking Stitches One Stitch at a Time a.k.a Tinking</u>

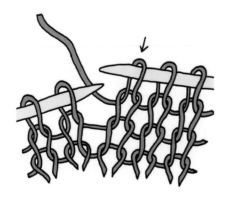

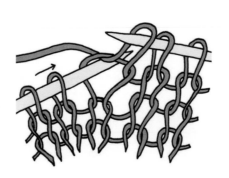

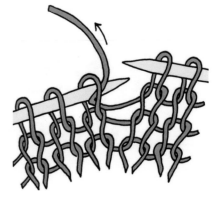

1. If you have made a mistake and just need to unpick (undo) a few stitches, this is a good way to do it! The arrow indicates which stitch is going to be unpicked.

2. Insert your left needle into the stitch below the one you have just knit from front to back as shown.

3. As you slide this stitch back onto your left needle, allow the yarn to drop out of it.

Frogging

Sometimes you don't see a mistake until several rows later and going all the way back to the point where the mistake was made is just what you have to do. Does it mean you might have to undo several hours worth of knitting to fix it? Yes. But it also means more quality time with your yarn. Cue up your favourite show and enjoy the satisfaction of getting those stitches right! Knitters like to call the process of removing several rows of stitches 'frogging'. The name comes from the fact that we say we are ripping back our stitches. We 'rip it, rip it' - sounds like 'ribbit', eh? Believe it or not, you can just whisk your needles out of your stitches and gently pull the yarn out, row by row. When you get to the mistake row, you can carefully unpick each stitch one by one, replacing them onto the needle as you go.

Knit How

LOVING STUFF

Caring for Your Knits

You learned to knit! You knit a scarf, a sock, a sweater, whatever! And you wore it! You may have even garnered a few compliments or elicited a "could you knit me a..." or two. Now that your knits have been out on the town, they'll need some TLC at home. Here are a few of our tips for keeping them shipshape for years to come.

Washing

Some knits, like a cowl or mittens, may never need washing. But even for the least sweaty of your knits, there's always the chance of a spilled cup of hot chocolate, or a bus driving through a dirty puddle at just the wrong moment. For handknits, washing is essentially the same process as blocking (described in Chapter 1 on page 35). Even when yarn is marketed as being 'superwash', meaning it is machine-washable, we are fans of hand washing. Many washing machines have knitwear cycles but we've seen far too many heartbreaking accidents to recommend relying on this. Warm water, strong detergents and the normal friction of the washing barrel can easily shrink or - worse - felt your handknit. We can't bear to think of you losing your beautiful knit that took so many hours to make, so why chance it?*

To recap, washing or blocking your knits involves giving them a lukewarm, sudsy bath using a no rinse wool wash, gently squeezing out the water, and laying the piece flat to dry, pinning if necessary to get it to the specified measurements. Most yarn shops sell a no rinse wool wash. If you can't get to a shop or find there are too many choices, then gentle Eucalan is a great brand to start with.

Storing

Your handknits are best kept folded in a drawer. Much as we'd love to see a beautiful line-up of sweaters in our wardrobes, hangers are really not their friends. Hangers will put an unnecessary strain on the shoulders of garments and cause the weight of the yarn to stretch the entire piece.

Many knitters are waging a constant battle with moths. If you live in a region where moths are rife, consider using a wool wash with lavender, or investing in sachets meant to deter moths. Moths especially love knitwear that the wearer has sweat into; all the more reason to keep your knits nice and wash them now and again. If you have a very serious moth problem, you may want to store your knits (and even your yarn!) in airtight plastic bags or containers.

De-pilling

Over time, you may notice little bobbly pills appear on your handknits, especially in places where there is extra friction, like on the underside of sleeves, where your arms rub against your body. The softer your yarn is, the more likely pills will happen. Don't stress though, your sweater isn't ruined, it just needs some love! There are a number of handy tools you can use to remove them. Battery-operated pill shavers are great, as are tools like the Gleener which are marketed specifically to handknitters. In a pinch, a razor will do the trick; just be careful!

*There are exceptions to our hand wash only rule, for example knits made of cotton or linen, which can often benefit from a good machine wash!

Part 4

WHERE TO NEXT?

WHERE TO NEXT?

This book was designed to give you a good grounding in the world of knitting. We hope that you've made a number of successful projects that you and your loved ones enjoy wearing! The more you knit, the better you'll get. We find that almost every new project builds your skills and confidence as a knitter, regardless of how long you've been knitting. When you're ready to branch out from the projects in this book, and even before, we highly recommend that you join us and over eight million other knitters on the knitting social network, Ravelry.com. It is so much more than just a social network; it is a library and database of thousands of knitting patterns, as well as forums where knitters (and crocheters and weavers) can ask questions, chat, and share their own projects with others who will appreciate them! We have our own group and forum on Ravelry.com, appropriately called Pom Pom. We and our friendly group members are there ready to give advice and admire your finished projects, so please do join us!

Ready, Set, Go!

So how do you decide what to knit next? You might see something in a shop you'd like to try yourself, or perhaps you'll be inspired to try something you've spotted in a knitting magazine! Whatever gets you going, you might want to gauge how much of a challenge you're up for with your next project. As we mentioned before, Ravelry.com is an excellent resource to explore knitting patterns because other knitters have already rated the pattern based on difficulty and they often share tips to make things easier. This will help you get a feel for whether it's the right project for you or not.

Often, whether or not you're ready to knit something depends on what kind of personality you have. If you see an intricately cabled sweater and are up for the challenge, we won't stop you! But if you're more of a 'slow and steady wins the race' type, there's no shame in taking baby steps with each new project. Even making the same thing a few times over can teach you a lot, so just go with what feels comfortable for you.

No matter where your knitting takes you next, just keep in mind that it's meant to be fun. Like most skills worth acquiring, knitting comes with challenges. If ever you feel stuck or discouraged, go to your local shop's knit night, sign up for a class, meet a knitting friend, or go online for support, encouragement, and abundant good knitting vibes. Always remember our ultimate Top Tip: the beauty of knitting is that you can always unravel and start fresh! Your gentle yarn will always be patient and happy to see you.

Abbreviations

beg	Beginning
cast off	Bind off
dec	Decrease
DPN(s)	Double-pointed needle(s)
foll	Follow(s)/Following
G st	Garter stitch
inc	Increase
k	Knit
kwise	As if to knit
k2tog	Knit 2 stitches together
LH	Left hand
M1L	Make 1 Left; pick up strand between the two needles from the front to back with the tip of left needle, knit into the back of this stitch
M1R	Make 1 Right; pick up strand between the two needles from back to front with the tip of left needle, knit into the front of this stitch
patt	Pattern
PM	Place marker
p	Purl
pwise	As if to purl
p2tog	Purl 2 stitches together
rem	Remain(s)/Remaining
rep	Repeat
rev St st	Reverse Stocking stitch (stockinette): purl on RS rows, knit on WS rows
RH	Right hand
RS	Right side of fabric
sl	Slip
ssk	Slip 2 stitches knitwise one at a time, knit together through the back loops
SM	Slip marker
st(s)	Stitch(es)

St st	Stocking stitch (stockinette): knit on RS rows, purl on WS rows
tbl	Through the back loop
tog	Together
wyib	With yarn held in back of work
wyif	With yarn held in front of work
WS	Wrong side of fabric
yo	Yarn over needle and into working position

Find more at *pompommag.com/tutorials*

Weighing Up The (Yarny) Options

Frequently used names for yarn weights and their overseas equivalents - a handy guide when substituting yarns!

UK	US	Recommended Needle Size
2ply	Laceweight	1.5-2.25mm / US 0-1
4ply/Fingering	4ply/Fingering	2.25-3.25mm / US 1-3
4ply/Fingering	Sock	2.25-3.25mm / US 1-3
In between a heavy 4ply & light DK	Sport	3.25-3.75mm / US 3-5
DK	DK/Light Worsted	3.75-4.5mm / US 5-7
Aran	Worsted	4.5-5.5mm / US 7-9
Chunky	Bulky	5.5-8mm / US 9-13
Super Chunky	Super Bulky	8mm+ / US 13

Knitter Lingo

Phrases and abbreviations you can start using at your LYS and on Ravelry.com like a pro.

FO — Finished Object

Frog — Undo large portions (or the entirety) of your work, so named because in order to undo it you have to 'rip it' back, and if you're undoing a lot of work you 'rip it, rip it, rip it...' etc. Which sounds like ribbit (the noise that frogs make)!

KAL — Knit-a-long - when a group of knitters knit the same project at the same time as each other, and share their progress. Often hosted on *Ravelry.com*, or via social media.

Lifeline — Waste yarn threaded through a row of stitches so that if any mistakes are made it's easy to undo work to that point.

LYS — Local Yarn Shop / Store

Muggle — Non-knitter

Second Sock Syndrome — Knitting one sock and then never quite getting around to finishing the second one.

Startitis — Beginning several projects in quick succession but not making progress on them before starting the next.

Stash — Yarn awaiting a future project.

Tink — Tink is 'knit' spelled backwards. It refers to undoing stitches by reversing the knitting motion - see page 148 for unpicking stitches one stitch at a time, which is the same thing!

UFO — Unfinished Object

Yarn Barf — A clump of yarn that comes out of a new ball of yarn when you pull from the centre of the ball.

WIP — Work In Progress

Yarn Chicken — When you are coming to the end of a project and running out of yarn, you are playing yarn chicken. Will the knitter win or will the yarn run out?

Knit How

Yarn Support

Here's a handy list of the yarns we used in this book and where to get them. Can't find one of these yarns near you? Have a look at our substitutions guide on the opposite page for help on choosing an alternative.

The Uncommon Thread
Merino DK
theuncommonthread.co.uk

Malabrigo
Chunky
malabrigoyarn.com

John Arbon Textiles
Viola
jarbon.com

BC Garn
Semilla Grosso
bcgarn.dk

Quince & Co.
Osprey
quinceandco.com

Retrosaria
Beiroa
retrosaria.rosapomar.com

De Rerum Natura
Gilliatt
dererumnatura.fr

Madelinetosh
Tosh DK
Madelinetosh.com

Green Mountain Spinnery
Mountain Mohair
spinnery.com

Coop Knits
Socks Yeah! DK
coopknits.co.uk

Julie Asselin
Nurtured
julie-asselin.com

Substituting Yarns

There are many reasons to try a different yarn than the one called for in the pattern: geography, colour, and fibre are all good reasons to deviate from what's prescribed. Here's our handy guide to changing things up.

1. Use the metre per gram rule, also known as the yard per ounce rule. Have a look at your pattern and see how many metres there are in the ball. As an example, there might be 80 metres per 50 gram ball. When choosing a substitute, go for a yarn that has a very similar number of metres per gram, or yards per ounce as the case may be.

2. Think about usage. It's unlikely that you'll want cotton mittens because cotton will stretch and won't keep you very warm. So think about where and how your knitted item will be used. If you're knitting a sweater for your friend in Norway, it's a good idea to use warming wool. If you're making a cardigan for your cousin who lives in Florida, you could consider a cotton blend.

3. Give thought to drape and weight. The easiest thing to do when substituting yarns is to stick to the same fibre content as the original. You'll find fibre content information on the yarn label. Wool usually has springy properties whereas, an alpaca and silk blend will usually be drapey and can stretch with wear. This can be beautiful when the pattern is designed to accommodate drape. But if you swap wool for alpaca in a pattern that doesn't accommodate it, you might find yourself with a cardigan much longer than you intended it to be after a few wears. Eventually you will become more familiar with how different fibres behave, but if you want to play it safe for now, go with the recommended fibre to avoid unpleasant surprises!

ACKNOWLEDGEMENTS

The making of *Knit How* was a truly collaborative effort with the entire Pom Pom team: Amy, Sophie, Francesca, Gayle, and Iesha were, as always, truly indispensable.

Alice Sleight was our compass in finally getting this book out into the world.

We are so grateful to honorary Pom Pom team members Francesca Hughes and Fiona Alice for lending their talents to the designs in this book.

Juju Vail is always our knitting guru and was so helpful with the beginning stages of *Knit How*.

We are forever appreciative of our skilled Technical Editors, Jemima Bicknell and Laura Chau, as well as Rachel Atkinson who edited many of the first pattern drafts. We are also so grateful to Annie Prime for her way with editing words.

We couldn't have made this book without Mary and Dan of Bless who brought it to life in all its colourful glory. We want to thank them for their zen-like patience, their knit book know-how, and for coming up with the name *Knit How*.

Many thanks to Hill Country Weavers in Austin, Texas, who lent their beautiful shop for some of the photography in this book. Speaking of beautiful yarn shops, we are indebted to Loop in London, where we first met, and were able to be inspired, teach, and fully immerse ourselves in the yarn world on a daily basis.

Meghan would like to specifically thank Janet Ziros, who taught her to knit when she was 16.

Lydia would like to thank Jess Wong who inspired her to pick up knitting, the rainy Welsh summer that kept her indoors long enough to get the hang of it, and her mum Sarah who wore some of her first knits even though they weren't very good.

To be able to write a book that welcomes new knitters into our woolly world is such an honour. We'd like to thank you for buying this book. We hope that knitting brings as much joy to your lives as it has to ours.

INDEX

INDEX